LINCOLN AND SLAVERY

LINCOLN AND SLAVERY

by Peter Burchard

ATHENEUM BOOKS FOR YOUNG READERS

Atheneum Books for Young Readers
An imprint of Simon & Schuster Children's Publishing Division
1230 Avenue of the Americas
New York, New York 10020

Book design by Angela Carlino

The text of this book is set in Adobe Garamond Regular.

Printed in the United States of America

10   9   8   7   6   5   4   3   2   1

Library of Congress Cataloging-in-Publication Data
Lincoln and slavery / Peter Burchard.—1st ed.
p.   cm.
Includes bibliographical references and index.
Summary: A biography of the sixteenth president which focuses on the issue of slavery and its importance throughout
Lincoln's life from his early days as a lawyer through his presidency.
ISBN 0-689-81570-0
1. Lincoln, Abraham, 1809-1865—Views on slavery—Juvenile literature. 2. Slaves—Emancipation—United States—
Juvenile literature. 3. Douglass, Frederick, 1818-1895—Juvenile literature. 4. United States—Politics and government—
1861-1865—Juvenile literature. 5. United States. Presidents (1861-1865: Lincoln). Emancipation Proclamation—
Juvenile literature. [1. Lincoln, Abraham, 1809-1865. 2. Presidents. 3. Slavery. 4. United States—Politics and
government—1861-1865.] I. Title.
E457.2.B96   1999
973.7'092—dc21   98-12464

FIRST
EDITION

For My Son

★ TABLE OF CONTENTS ★

ACKNOWLEDGMENTS

This book is dedicated to my son, without whose encouragement I might not have started it.

Thanks to Jane Poncia, whose constant and affectionate support helped me to reach what sometimes seemed a distant goal. Friend, writer, and historian Ormonde de Kay volunteered to read my manuscript and, in correcting and suggesting, helped make this a better book than it might otherwise have been. Thanks to editors Jonathan Lanman and Marcia Marshall for acceptance, sustenance, and sage advice.

The Williams College Sawyer Library provided me with all but two or three of the books listed in the bibliography. These included not only general works, but also published documents that one might expect to find only in remote and dusty places. Frederick Rudolph, who instituted a black studies program at Williams in 1965, is largely responsible for the Sawyer's excellent collection of materials on black history.

Many thanks to Williams College librarian Phyllis Cutler and her staff for their constant loyalty and help. Thanks to the reference team at the Sawyer: Lee Dalzell, Peter Giordano, Christine Menard, Rebecca Spencer, and Helena Warburg; as well as circulation supervisor Jo-Ann Irace and her staff, Linda Hall, Shirley Fitzpatrick, and Susan LeFaver. A special vote of thanks to Walter Komorowski, whose capacity to navigate among the rocks and shoals of the not always tranquil Sea of Electronic Resources never ceases to delight me. Thanks also to Robert Volz, custodian of the Williams College Chapin Library, for providing me with information I could not have found elsewhere.

My friend Donald Yacovone, one of several editors of *The Black Abolitionist Papers,* played an important, if sometimes contrary, role in helping me to shape a realistic view of Lincoln.

Thanks to librarian and friend James Cubit for unlocking doors for me in Illinois. Keepers of the flame in Springfield helped me more than I can say. At the Illinois State Historical Library, research specialist Kim Bauer and curator Mary Michals were especially helpful, as was Tim Goode at the Lincoln Home. In New Salem, several members of the staff encouraged me to warm my hands in front of open fires while they told me charming stories about Lincoln's residence in the little settlement—long since reconstructed and now maintained by the Illinois Historic Preservation Agency.

Last, but by no means least, thanks to Allan Heyward who, several years ago, gave me an extended tour of Richmond, Virginia, which—from 1861–1865—was the capital of the Confederate States of America.

INTRODUCTION

In New York, on the evening of February 27, 1860, a ten-year-old girl, who became my maternal grandmother, walked with her parents from their house on West Tenth Street to Cooper Square. There, she caught a glimpse of Lincoln as he stepped down from his carriage and went into Cooper Institute—now called Cooper Union. Her parents didn't take her in to hear his speech, but she learned later that it won him instant recognition in the East and sent him on his way to the White House. It was she who taught me to love Lincoln.

In my youth, I happily embraced what had become the Lincoln myth. Later, when I learned about his early compromises over slavery, I found excuses for him. When I heard what he said about the possibility of segregation of the races, I was as uncomfortable as I was when I read examples of his careless lapses into backwoods language, his use of words that today would be unacceptable. It saddened me to learn that, until two years or so before his death, he promoted the almost universal belief that black people were inherently inferior to those of other races.

What saved the day for me was the discovery that Lincoln, who was treated sternly, sometimes harshly, by his father, nonetheless found himself tortured by the memory of men in chains. It was comforting to learn that, whatever slang he used, he seldom talked down to a black man or black woman, that as president he appealed to black leader Frederick Douglass for advice.

All his life, Lincoln demonstrated a capacity to grow. He taught himself to read and write, to speak effectively, to practice law, to become a skillful politician. Not long after his first inauguration—on March 4, 1861—Douglass said of him, "The President is tall and strong but he is not done growing."

As Douglass, in his wisdom, made this prophecy, even he could not have guessed what giant steps the President was still to take. The last few years of Lincoln's life were marked by growth so dramatic as to make what went before seem no more than the progress of a natural genius toward an educated state.

I have always wished that I could talk to Lincoln, ask him questions, listen to him, wished that I could get acquainted with the flawed and complicated man behind the myth. In writing this short book about a crucial facet of his life, I have at least begun that conversation.

Peter Burchard
WILLIAMSTOWN, MASSACHUSETTS

"We were watching, as it were, by the dim light of the stars, for the dawn of a new day. . . ."

—Frederick Douglass

★ 1 ★

FATHER ABRAHAM IS COME!

After parts of the Confederate capital at Richmond had been burned and its several bridges wrecked by its own retreating soldiers, Lincoln paid a visit to the city.

On April 4, 1865, the *River Queen*, escorted by a tug and three warships, carried him and his son Tad up the James River to a point where pilings—driven into the soft riverbed to protect the city from amphibious attack—stopped the progress of the steamer.

Admiral David Porter, who had gone to Richmond earlier, came down to meet the president. With the help of several sailors, Lincoln and his son stepped aboard Porter's barge. First towed by the tug, then rowed by twelve oarsmen, the barge made its way up the James.

Smoke still hung above the city, a reminder of the danger lurking in the streets and alleyways occupied by Union troops the day before. The barge

OPPOSITE: Lincoln in 1846, four years after he was married. This image and the 1846 photograph of Mary on page 12 were probably the work of N. H. Shepherd, one of Springfield's first photographers. *Williams College Sawyer Library*

docked at a landing just above Libby Prison, which had held several hundred prisoners of war.

Tad may have been allowed to accompany his father as a celebration of his twelfth birthday. The boy was small for his age and, born with crooked teeth and a cleft palate, spoke with a nasal lisp. There were times when only Lincoln understood him. Lincoln, who loved and indulged his sons, held Tad's hand as they walked with Admiral Porter and their guards up a steep rutted lane on their way to the mansion that had served as the Confederate White House and was, by then, the headquarters of the ranking Union officers.

The day was fine. Off to the west, where the smoke had blown away, the sky was blue. A young Massachusetts soldier wrote admiringly that spring weather touched Virginia with a splendor greater than New England ever saw. Word of

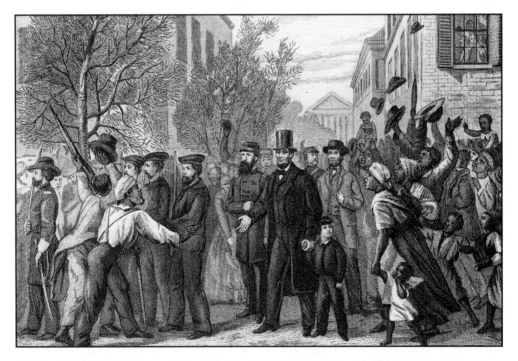

On April 4, 1865, Lincoln and his son Tad walked through the streets of Richmond, Virginia, which had, for four years, been the capital of the Confederacy. There, they were greeted by black people freed the day before. *Library of Congress*

the president's arrival spread throughout the black community. People lined the curbstones, shouting joyously, reaching out to touch his hand or the fabric of his sleeve. Someone called, "Bless the Lord. Father Abraham is come!" A gray-haired man, who was working by the roadside, dropped his shovel and shouted, "Glory Hallelujah!" When he kneeled in front of Lincoln and bent down to kiss his dusty, square-toed shoes, Lincoln told him, "You must kneel to God only."

Lincoln's journey from his birthplace in Kentucky to the streets of Richmond had been long and tortuous. He was born on February 12, 1809, in a log cabin near Hodgenville. His parents, poor and illiterate, were opposed to slavery. As a child, he saw so few black people that he never quite forgot a black woman who gave him a glass of milk while his family was engaged in a bitter winter's trek to a rise of ground near Little Pigeon Creek, in Indiana, where they had decided to resettle.

Lincoln's mother died when he was nine, but his father soon married again, and his stepmother loved him and encouraged in him a great purity of spirit. Lincoln might have heard his elders talk about the Missouri Compromise of 1820–21, which admitted Maine as a free state and Missouri as a slave state, but in childhood he gave little thought to slavery.

When he was nineteen, with a friend named Allen Gentry, Lincoln made a 1,200-mile journey down the Ohio and Mississippi rivers on a flatboat carrying a load of produce to New Orleans. The two young men traveled mostly in the daytime, anchoring or docking at sundown. One night, when they were docked just below Baton Rouge and were sleeping, seven black men came aboard. Years later, Lincoln wrote that their intention was to "kill and rob," that he and his mate "were hurt some in the melee." Here, Lincoln's great height and extraordinary strength enabled him and his friend to drive away their attackers, cast off, and pole away into the swift river current. Most young men in Lincoln's time would have blamed the brutality of the marauders on their racial origins. Lincoln showed no such prejudice.

On March 1, 1830, when he was twenty-one, he moved, with his family, from Indiana to a stretch of land ten miles west of Decatur, Illinois; but when his family moved again—this time east to Coles County—he decided he would stay behind.

In the spring of 1831, following a second voyage down the Mississippi, he was in New Orleans long enough to explore the city. To the rawboned, slightly awkward country youth, it might as well have been a European seaport. The buildings in the Vieux Carré—the French Quarter—were like nothing he had seen before, and the docks and thoroughfares were alive with sailors speaking French and Spanish and exotic local dialects. On streets leading northwest from the steamy waterfront, there were showrooms where slaves were on display. In the city's marketplaces, slaves were sold in much the same manner as were animals, bales of cotton, and casks of rum.

In New Orleans, Lincoln must have seen slaves in chains and slaves being sold. As novelist Harriet Beecher Stowe would illustrate in *Uncle Tom's Cabin*—published in 1852—one of the tragic aspects of the sale of slaves was the splitting up of families. On auction blocks, men and women lost their children and grandchildren, lost each other, aunts and uncles and close friends, never to set eyes on them again. In slave markets, beautiful young women were stripped, prodded, and sold to the owners of New Orleans pleasure palaces or to rough and heartless planters.

Back in central Illinois, Lincoln lived in New Salem—a village on a bluff above the Sangamon River. There he worked, at one thing and another, and won the respect and admiration of his neighbors.

As he settled in New Salem, his countrymen were beginning to respond to a growing group of men and women who insisted that they pay attention to the immorality of slavery. In the Northeast, abolitionists like Benjamin Lundy, Charles G. Finney, Theodore Weld, Lewis Tappan, and William Lloyd Garrison were agitating for the immediate release of slaves in all states and territories, North and South. It was, to say the least, unrealistic to expect plantation owners, whose privileged way of life depended on the continuance of slavery, to give in to reformers—most of whom were living in New England—but they were sensitive to criticism and became increasingly rebellious. Even in the 1830s, there were Southerners who talked about secession—separation from the Union.

Log houses in New Salem, Illinois, as they appear today. Lincoln lived in the lofts of several houses in the village. The village was abandoned shortly after Lincoln left it. It was later reconstructed and is now maintained by the Illinois Historic Preservation Agency. *Photograph by the author*

Lincoln always was what he called "naturally Anti-slavery." But as he worked as a storekeeper and surveyor and served as a captain in the Black Hawk War—a war waged essentially to subdue the native population—he saw few, if any, slaves and seldom thought of slavery. He did, however, often speak out for the underdog, and during his brief service in the Black Hawk War, he saved the life of an aged Indian. When the man stumbled into Lincoln's camp, some of Lincoln's men suggested hanging him. One said, "The Indian is a damned spy. . . . We have come out to fight the Indian and by God we intend to do so."

Lincoln, tall and unyielding, stood by the frightened man, threatened to fight anyone who laid a hand on him, gave him food, and let him go.

While he lived in New Salem—between 1831 and 1837—Lincoln took an interest in the law, which was to be his most essential tool in his campaign against slavery. He began to read law books. Soon, he was a familiar figure in courthouses in his neighborhood. He talked to lawyers and to judges, listened to their arguments.

Lincoln aimed to practice law not only as a clever way of making money, but also because of his devotion to his freedom and the freedom of his neighbors. He read at least part of the *Revised Statutes of Indiana,* the preface of which contained the texts of the Declaration of Independence and the Constitution of the United States.

He probably read very little of the Indiana code, but his first careful study of Thomas Jefferson's Declaration brought a sense of recognition and enlightenment to the young, self-educated man. Most important was the phrase "all men are created equal." To him, this meant that all men and women must be equal under law, that all must have *an equal chance.* It meant that a person's race—his features and the color of his skin—could not make him a *thing* that might be bought and sold. Lincoln's study of the Declaration led him to believe that his nation had a global mission, that Jefferson had given liberty not only to the people of his country, but "hope to all the world, for all future time."

As a young man, Lincoln learned that every law passed in the states and territories and by Congress must be found in the United States Constitution. But the trouble with the Constitution was that, when delegates from twelve states met in Philadelphia in 1787 and began to draft the document, slavery was, as it were, a serpent, coiled and sleeping underneath the conference table.

The first slaves of African origin had been landed in Jamestown, Virginia, in 1619—a year before the arrival of the *Mayflower,* 113 years before George Washington was born, and 246 years before ratification, on December 6, 1865, of the Thirteenth Amendment to the Constitution, which abolished slavery "within the United States, or any place subject to their jurisdiction."

By 1787, slavery had long been established in America, and colonials—including many of the founding fathers—were slaveholders. So, after long and passionate debate, the Constitution was composed without repudiation of the country's greatest evil. Slavery was never mentioned in the document, but, in a sly and shameful compromise, it gave slaveholders a conspicuous advantage in the Congress. In a Congress that was made up of two houses—called "bicameral"—each state, regardless of its population, was represented by two senators, but the number of its legislators in the House of Representatives was determined by its population. The Constitution—as first written and with no amendments—stated that the population of a state would be determined by adding to the number of free persons in the state "three-fifths of all other persons." These other persons were, of course, large numbers of black people held in bondage. Though no slave could vote for any legislator or, in fact, for anyone, he was counted as three-fifths of a man and, in effect, helped to send a representative to Congress who would vote for the continuance and spread of slavery.

Some of the framers of the Constitution believed that slavery would wither

Illustration of a slave auction, in Charleston, South Carolina. The sale of slaves was commonplace in the Americas for two hundred years or more, at first in both North and South. From *The Illustrated London News*, November 29, 1856. *Schomburg Center for Research in Black Culture*

on the vine, as it had in other countries. They were wrong. Slaves cultivated cotton. An increase in textile manufacture—together with the appearance of the cotton gin*—marked the beginning of the dominance of cotton in world markets. A greater demand for cotton led directly to the spread of slavery.

Short and general as it is, the Constitution can be taken to mean many different, and sometimes opposing, things. Lincoln's study of the document led him to believe that the federal government had no power to abolish slavery in states where it had long been established. He continued to believe this until a rebellion of the Southern states enabled him to change the rules.

Above all other threats to American democracy, Lincoln feared the spread of slavery. He knew that energetic young Americans were heading west, pushing back and killing off the native population, clearing land, cultivating virgin soil. If something wasn't done to stop the spread of slavery, it would accompany or follow after settlement and would overwhelm democracy.

Aside from founding documents, the young Lincoln's most important source was a worn set of Sir William Blackstone's *Commentaries on the Laws of England*—first published in 1765. Because most U.S. law was based on the laws of England, Lincoln gave close attention to the work. He said later that he went at it "good and earnest." From Blackstone, Lincoln learned that common law encouraged ordinary people to be fair to one another. Blackstone gave Lincoln an increased respect for history. From the Englishman, Lincoln learned that law had been constructed like a great cathedral, that it was a building always rising, never finished.

Lincoln may or may not have known that orator, politician, and philosopher Marcus Tullius Cicero, who had lived almost two thousand years before, had proclaimed, "It is not possible for the people of Rome to be slaves, whom the gods have destined to command all nations. Other nations may endure slavery, but the proper end and business of the Roman people is liberty!" In any case, Lincoln learned that humankind had hungered after liberty long

---

* Patented by Eli Whitney in 1794, the device made it possible to separate rapidly the fiber of short staple cotton from its seed.

before the birth of Thomas Jefferson and that otherwise despotic leaders had at least frowned on slavery. Blackstone wrote, "Liberty by the English law depends not upon the complexion; and what was said even in the time of Queen Elizabeth, is now substantially true, that the air of England is too pure for a slave to breathe it."

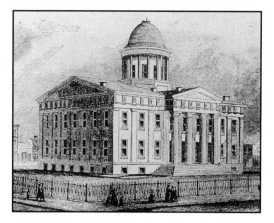

The Illinois State Capitol as it was in the nineteenth century. The building, which has been restored, is now much as it was in Lincoln's day. *Courtesy of Lincoln Home National Historic Park*

In 1834—when he was twenty-five—Lincoln was elected to the Illinois House of Representatives, where he was to serve four terms, first in Vandalia, then, after the state capital was moved, in Springfield. By 1836, when he was elected to the Bar of Illinois, law was to him what religion was to many of his compatriots.

Lincoln's way with people, his uncompromising honesty, his good nature, and his sense of humor—together with his knowledge of the law—enabled him to become a successful politician. As a young legislator, he was increasingly aware of the activities of abolitionists, especially those in the Midwest. In 1837, one of these—Elijah P. Lovejoy, who had come west from Maine—was killed in Alton, Missouri, near St. Louis.

Lovejoy was the publisher of the *Alton Observer*. Though he did not declare himself an abolitionist, he hated slavery and expressed antislavery sentiments. His brother's house, in Alton, was a stop along the Underground Railroad—a chain of hideouts where courageous men and women gave food, shelter, and directions to escaping slaves.

The atmosphere in the town was anything but healthy. In the spring of 1836, proslavery men had chained and burned a free black man named Francis McIntosh who had been accused of murder, and had stoned his lifeless body. Lovejoy had been threatened many times, and his wife was terrified. He had every reason to leave town, but, ignoring his wife's state of mind, he proclaimed that he feared God more than he feared any man.

Three of Lovejoy's presses had been wrecked by racist mobs and sunk in the Mississippi River. When his fourth press was delivered to him, on November 7, 1837, he decided to protect it with his life. That evening, with a company of sympathizers—armed with muskets, clubs, and pistols—he stood guard in a fieldstone warehouse that contained his newsroom and pressroom.

Outside, moonlight was reflected in the waters of the Mississippi. Soon, a mob of about one hundred men approached the building. As one of the invaders threatened to break down a door, he was shot and killed by one of Lovejoy's men.

The attackers, temporarily intimidated, fell back, gathered, and withdrew to a saloon. When they came back, several of them put a ladder up against a wall of Lovejoy's building, then retreated; when Lovejoy went outside to knock the ladder down, he was hit by musket fire. As he staggered back inside, he clutched at his chest and whispered, "I am shot. I am shot."

The news of Lovejoy's death spread far and wide. A gathering of black people in New York passed a resolution

> That the blood of the martyred Lovejoy calls upon us, an oppressed people, to become more united in sentiment and efforts, while two and a half millions of our brethren are dragging out a life of misery and degradation in that most detestable system of slavery which not only reduces its victims to brutes, but threatens slavery and death to those who plead their cause. . . . That among our rights, we hold none dearer than the freedom of speech and of the press.

Before the funeral, Owen Lovejoy, kneeling by his brother's body, made a vow: "I shall never forsake the cause that has been sprinkled with my brother's blood."

Lincoln was in Springfield when he heard the news of Lovejoy's death. He was touched by the loss of a man so dedicated and was firm in his defense of civil liberties. Honoring the first ten amendments to the Constitution, which constitute the Bill of Rights, he said that abolitionists must be free to congregate and speak their minds, free to publish their opinions.

William H. Herndon—a young law student who, in 1844, would become Lincoln's law partner—tells us that, not long after Lovejoy's death, he went to church with Lincoln. The preacher, Peter Akers, must have had the martyred Lovejoy on his mind, because he read from the book of Zechariah of prophecies and trouble and eventual redemption. Slavery, he told his congregation, was the trouble with America. He predicted that the evil would be conquered sometime in the 1860s. Then, as the congregation rose to sing a hymn, he remarked, "Who can tell but that the man who shall lead us through this strife may be standing in our presence?"

After the service ended, Lincoln sat in silence until someone asked him how he liked the sermon. Lincoln said that it was the most impressive sermon he had ever heard. Herndon would write later that, thereafter, Lincoln believed "that a peculiar work and an important destiny awaited him."

Following a stormy courtship, Lincoln married Mary Todd on November 4, 1842. On Mary's gold wedding band was engraved the sentiment, "Love is eternal."

Lincoln and his wife both belonged to the Whig party. Following his marriage, Lincoln took an increasing interest in his party's principles—the promotion of the growth of industry in the Northeast, of farming in the South and West, and the linking of all sections of the country by an efficient railway system.

Lincoln soon set his sights on election to the the U.S. House of Representatives. He wrote to newspaper editors, influential members of his party, and his friends, making his intentions known and promising to support the party's programs. He was nominated by acclamation and ran against itinerant preacher Peter Cartwright. Elected on August 3, 1846, Lincoln had a year to prepare to go to Washington.

LEFT: Mary Lincoln in 1846. Mary loved the early photographs. She said that this one was taken "when we were young and so desperately in love." *Library of Congress*

BELOW: The Globe Tavern, in Springfield, Illinois. Here Lincoln started married life. Here Mary gave birth to their first son, Robert Todd. *Williams College Sawyer Library*

✭ 2 ✭

THE ROOT OF THE TROUBLES

Lincoln, Mary, and their two sons, Robert and Edward, left Springfield on November 25, 1847. They probably went by stagecoach, then by rail, to Harpers Ferry, changed cars, and went on to Washington. They arrived December 2, in the evening, stayed first in Brown's Hotel, and later moved to Mrs. Ann Sprigg's boardinghouse.

In Lincoln's day, the streets of Washington were muddy thoroughfares, paved here and there with cobblestones. Most sidewalks were no more than earthen footpaths, some of them overlaid with rough pine boards. The capital was essentially a Southern city. It was a crossroads of slavery. Slaves were jailed, bought, and sold within hailing distance of the White House. Adult white men who called each other "boys" roamed the streets, tormenting free black people, hunting slaves who had escaped—most of them from slave owners in Maryland and Virginia—and picking fights with Yankee visitors and congressmen.

Mrs. Sprigg's establishment consisted of an assortment of bedrooms, each equipped with a washstand and a large white china pitcher filled with water

The chamber of the House of Representatives as it was sixteen years before Lincoln served a term as a U.S. Congressman from Illinois. *Library of Congress*

drawn from a well. The four Lincolns stayed together in a large upstairs room. Several guests shared one of three or four bathrooms. At mealtimes, boarders gathered in a common dining room. Black men waited on the tables. Probably unknown to Mrs. Sprigg, and certainly unknown to Lincoln, one of these was a slave who was paying his master in installments for his freedom.

All her life, Mary Lincoln suffered from depression. She was moody, often difficult. In an age when only half the country's children reached adulthood, Edward was a sickly babe in arms. Robert, who was not yet four, was undisciplined and made a nuisance of himself. At first, Mary liked the city but, in time, grew tired of it and, in the spring 1848, took her children to her father's house in Kentucky, leaving Lincoln to devote himself to his duties in the Congress.

Also living in Mrs. Sprigg's boardinghouse was Ohio Congressman Joshua R. Giddings—a consistent abolitionist—and several other antislavery congressmen. Lincoln befriended Giddings but soon saw that, while Giddings was a man of principle, he was not an effective legislator. In fact, with one exception, Lincoln found the men who were serving in the House with him uninspiring. The exception was short, gimlet-eyed John Quincy Adams, who had been a senator, a minister to Russia, Great Britain, and the Hague, and the sixth president of the United States. Instead of leaving government in 1828 when he was not reelected president, he had chosen to live out his life as a Massachusetts congressman and, as such, became his nation's first, and perhaps its greatest, antislavery legislator.

In 1832, in conversation with Alexis de Tocqueville, Adams talked about the clear threat of slavery to democracy. Tocqueville, a young Frenchman who was touring North America, asked him, "Do you look on slavery as a great plague for the United States?"

"Yes. Certainly," Adams answered. "That is the root of almost all the troubles of the present and fears for the future."

Adams was first to assert the right of the federal government to set slaves free in time of war. He said, "From the instant your slave-holding states become a theater of war—civil, servile or foreign—from that instant the war powers of the Constitution extend to interference with the institution of slavery in every way that it can be interfered with."

John Quincy Adams as he was in his seventies, when he was serving as a Congressman from Massachusetts. As a young man in the eighteenth century, he was slim and handsome and wore a powdered wig and ruffled stock. Adams was a President of the United States, a senator, and an Ambassador to Russia, Great Britain, and the Hague. Throughout his life, he was consistently opposed to slavery. From an engraving from a painting by Asher Brown Durand. *Williams College Sawyer Library*

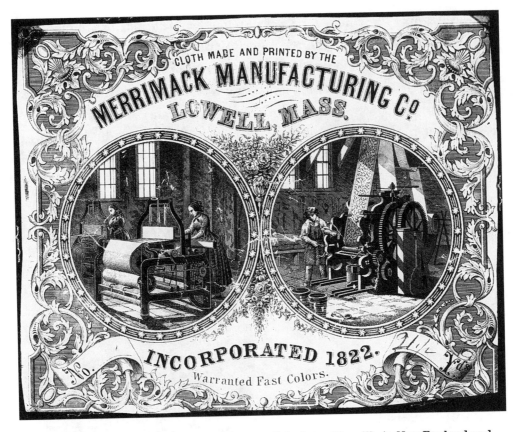

For forty years or more before slavery was abolished, textile mills in New England and in England increasingly relied on cotton grown by slave labor in the South. As a result, most New Englanders openly supported slavery. *Smithsonian Institution*

Here, Adams was referring not just to civil wars and wars with foreign powers, but to wars of liberation started by slaves themselves. Lincoln's Emancipation Proclamation, composed in 1862, was to echo this clear declaration.

When Lincoln joined the Congress, a fault line divided North and South. Plantation owners in the South—whose most profitable crop was cotton—had long prospered from the toil of their several million slaves. While plantations in the valleys and rich coastal regions of the South were worked by slaves, the rocky soil of the Northeastern states was cultivated by its owners. While they worked their fields and took care of their livestock, enterprising businessmen in the North made large sums of money in shipbuilding, trade with China, and investment in steel mills, railroads, and manufacturing.

As Lincoln hung his hat in his nation's capital, slavery had long since been outlawed in New England and in what had been the Middle Colonies—New York, Pennsylvania, and New Jersey; but, with few exceptions, free black people lived and worked at the bottom of the social scale, and in cities in the North, prejudice against them often brought on vicious race riots in which many lost their lives.

One of Lincoln's great concerns was the link between the plantations of the South and the factories of the North. New England textile mills used large amounts of cotton, as did the mills in England—most of them in Manchester. Cotton was a binding economic force at the same time that slavery was undermining the foundations of American democracy. Cotton—together with rice, tobacco, and indigo—was so important that, when at last the Civil War was under way and Union forces were about to occupy the Sea Islands of South Carolina, Georgia, and Florida, Southerners had trouble believing that the federal government would be so foolish as to interfere with so valuable a harvest. One planter asked, "Would any sane nation make war on cotton?"

Henry Clay and John Quincy

Henry Clay in middle age. Born in 1777, he was for more than twelve years Speaker of the House of Representatives. He also served as Secretary of State, was a candidate for president, and was a U.S. senator. Clay was, for many years, Lincoln's model. His thirty years of compromise over slavery postponed what William Seward called an irrepressible conflict—the Civil War. From an engraving from a portrait by Savinien E. Dubourjal. *Williams College Sawyer Library*

Adams had founded the Whig Party in 1834 to oppose what they thought of as the "reckless tyranny" of military hero Andrew Jackson. For forty years, Clay had been a leading statesman, congressman, senator, and presidential candidate. He was a slave owner who believed that slavery must be phased out. He was a compromiser who, in several times of crisis, had helped keep the Union from disintegrating. He was not in Washington when Lincoln joined the Congress but, in 1849, was to be reelected to the Senate.

If most of Lincoln's fellow representatives were uninspiring, there were senators, besides Clay, who were legendary statesmen—among them Daniel Webster, John C. Calhoun, and Thomas Hart Benton. All three were lawyers, all three seasoned politicians. Like Lincoln, Webster hated slavery and believed in compromise. Calhoun defended and promoted slavery, while Benton—although born in Tennessee and living in Missouri—was also an antislavery legislator. These men, giants in their time, were growing old and would soon make way for younger men.

Among the senators who were close to Lincoln's age were Jefferson Davis, later to become president of the Confederacy, and Hannibal Hamlin, who was to be vice president under Lincoln. Illinois Senator Stephen A. Douglas, who was fast gaining power, had already faced Lincoln in debate in courts of law in Illinois and was to play a crucial role in his election to the presidency.

During his first session in the Congress, Lincoln took a stand on a subject that was fast becoming a dead issue. Democratic President James K. Polk was winding down a war with Mexico. Lincoln knew it was his duty to support his country's soldiers, but he thought of the Mexican adventure as no more than a grab for a neighbor's territory. In several speeches on the floor of the House, he criticized the president, saying that he had made an unprovoked attack on territory occupied by Mexico. In Washington, Lincoln's speeches on the war went unnoticed. In Illinois, they were called unpatriotic.

In Mrs. Sprigg's boardinghouse, Lincoln was an entertainer. At the supper table, he told rustic jokes and beguiled his fellow guests with stories of his prairie years. He expressed no interest in card games but went bowling with his fellow legislators. He defended freedom of religion but was seldom seen in church.

Sometimes, after supper, he walked alone in the streets of Washington. Having lived in Illinois, it must have seemed natural to him that not only dogs, but pigs and chickens foraged in the streets and alleyways. In warm weather, clouds of tobacco smoke and the sounds of raucous laughter radiated from the open doorways of the dozens of saloons that lined Pennsylvania Avenue, but these establishments failed to attract the congressman from Illinois. He had done a little drinking in his youth and remembered how it made him feel. Liquor, he said, left him "flabby and undone."

Close to the Capitol, he saw droves of black men living in what he described as a "sort of negro livery-stable." The building was the warehouse of Franklin & Armfield, where slaves, most of them en route to plantations in the South, were fed a tasteless gruel, given a short daily ration of polluted water, and made to sleep on a rough floor on thin scatterings of straw. Some died of malaria and were buried in a common grave.

Because Lincoln seldom spoke or wrote about his feelings, it is hard to measure the intensity of his attitude toward slavery as he served in the Congress. In his letters to his wife, whose parents in Kentucky were slave owners, he rarely mentioned slavery. Even in his letters to his friends, he seldom wrote about his discomfort over slavery; but he had once seen a sight that had later inspired him to take pen in hand. In a letter to his close friend Joshua Speed, whose people, like Mary's, were slave owners, he wrote, "In 1841, you and I had together a tedious low-water trip on a Steam-Boat from Louisville to St. Louis. You may remember, as I well do, that from Louisville to the mouth of the Ohio there were, on board, ten or a dozen slaves, shackled together with irons." At the time, Lincoln had remarked that the captives were the happiest of voyagers, but later on, in writing Speed, he revealed that he had long been brooding over the injustice of their plight. "That sight was a continual torment to me." He went on, "It is hardly fair for you to assume that I have no interest in a thing which has, and continually exercises, the power of making me miserable. You ought to appreciate how the great body of the Northern people do crucify their feelings, in order to maintain their loyalty to the Constitution and the Union."

Repeatedly, but with no enthusiasm, Lincoln voted for one version or another of the Wilmot Proviso, contrived by Pennsylvania's antislavery congressman, David Wilmot. Had it passed, the proviso would have outlawed slavery in Southwestern lands acquired in the war with Mexico. Lincoln's lack of passionate support for the measure stemmed not from its content, but from the futility of voting for it in a Congress dominated by slaveholders.

In the fall of 1848, Lincoln campaigned in the East for Whig presidential candidate Zachary Taylor. Mary and his sons joined Lincoln as he spoke in New England. Some of his listeners thought that he was spellbinding. Most reporters praised his clarity of thought. Others criticized his voice. In Worcester, Massachusetts, a reporter for the *Boston Daily Advertiser* wrote, "He spoke in a clean and cool and very eloquent manner." But another journalist remembered what he called Lincoln's awkward gestures and his "comical expression."

On December 7, 1848—three days late—he began his second and last session in the House of Representatives. During his first session, he had not only given his attention to the war with Mexico, but had encouraged government support for improvement of the nation's waterways, bridges, harbors, and highways. As promised, he had promoted the expansion of the nation's railway system.

In 1849, he renewed these efforts, but he and every other legislator knew they faced a bitter struggle over slavery. For the first time in his career, Lincoln gave more than passing thought to antislavery legislation.

As we have seen, abolitionists pointed out repeatedly that slavery was a moral outrage, a disgrace. If their language was excessively dramatic, it left their audience with vivid images. William Lloyd Garrison had said that "the blood of souls" was on the nation's garments. He praised the Declaration of Independence and, with equal fervor, damned the Constitution.

When Lincoln went to visit Mary's or Speed's people in Kentucky, he saw house servants and field hands, all of whom were in bondage but were treated with great kindness. Though he had seen slave markets and slave pens, he had not seen slavery on the large plantations of the South.

In the winter of 1838–1839, English actress Fanny Kemble—married to Pierce Butler, who was said to be a "good" master—wrote about what she saw on her husband's islands on the coast of Georgia. On a cold winter's day, Kemble visited sick women in a drafty building that was used as an infirmary. A flue was clogged, and all the rooms were filled with smoke. One woman, who was so sick that she could barely speak, told Kemble that she had nine children. "There she lay, a mass of filthy tatters, without so much as a blanket under her or over her, on the bare earth in the chilly darkness."

Kemble talked to other women who broke up the soil with hoes instead of plows because, as one of them explained, "Horses cost more to keep than colored folks." Kemble also heard about punishments meted out to female slaves who were fastened by their wrists to a high beam, so their toes just touched the ground. Their skirts were tied above their heads, and they were whipped with leather thongs.

English actress Fanny Kemble married slaveholder Pierce Butler in 1834 and, four years later, went with him to his plantation on the coast of Georgia. Her record of her visit, written in the form of letters to her friend Elizabeth Sedgwick, was published shortly after Lincoln issued his Emancipation Proclamation. So graphically did Kemble represent the reality of slavery that her book was, at first, widely read, but it never gained the attention it deserved. Photograph of a painting by Thomas Sully. *The collection of the author*

Since Kemble's journals weren't published until 1863, Lincoln probably never read them, but he had seen enough of slavery to share the pain and feel the anger of a people kept in bondage. He said that if slavery wasn't wrong, then nothing was.

Lincoln may or may not have been in Mrs. Sprigg's dining room when three armed men stormed in and arrested the black waiter who was working to secure his freedom. Lincoln must, at least, have heard about the incident. The waiter had only sixty dollars left to pay when his owner changed his mind, kept his money, and demanded his return to slavery.

There is no record of a link between this pitiful occurrence and Lincoln's drafting of a bill that would abolish slavery in the District of Columbia—which, unlike the states, was subject to the will of Congress. As far back as 1837, when he was serving in the Illinois state legislature, he had argued for the right of Congress to abolish slavery in the District, but the reenslavement of the servant in the boardinghouse must certainly have deepened Lincoln's sense of shame over slavery in his nation's capital.

In any case, consulting other legislators and administrators in the District, Lincoln worked on a bill that he believed would, in time, be effective. Congressman Giddings, in drafting a bill of his own, had given voting rights to free black people but had come to realize that any bill containing such a measure would be

When Lincoln served in the House of Representatives, Washington was a crossroads of slavery. Free black people lived in shanties such as these. This photograph, by Matthew Brady, was taken in 1860. *National Archives*

doomed, so he helped draft Lincoln's compromise. Lincoln specified that his bill must be voted on by the white people of the District, some of whom were slaveholders. Had it been introduced and passed, it would have liberated children born to slave mothers after January 1, 1850—putting liberated babies in the arms of captive mothers. The bill provided that slaveholders who were willing to give up their slaves would be promptly reimbursed for their loss of property.

Lincoln found some support for his bill, but no more than a glance at it infuriated Southerners. It irritated abolitionists, most of whom recognized that it was a comedy of compromise, so Lincoln never introduced it.

Agitation over slavery only stiffened the resistance of the Southern radicals. Men like Calhoun began to talk of slavery as "a positive good," insisting that it showered benefits on a people who would otherwise have lived as savages. Never mind that slaveholders actively prevented slaves from learning how to read and write, kept them from learning anything that might help them to be self-sufficient. Calhoun and his followers went so far as to propose a constitutional amendment declaring slavery legal in all states and territories.

The long string of attempted compromises over slavery did American democracy in general and Lincoln in particular little credit. Slavery was indefensible, but, because Southern pressures were relentless, efforts to contain it would continue to be useless; North and South would, at last, go to war.

On Monday, March 5, the day after Lincoln's second and last term in Congress ended, he attended the inaugural festivities for President Zachary Taylor. With his friend Elihu Washburne—soon to become a senator—he left the ball in the early hours of the morning. In the cloakroom, he couldn't find his hat. The hat was probably less expensive than those of most other congressmen, but, schooled as he had been in frugality, he didn't want to lose it. He and Washburne spent almost an hour looking for it, then gave up.

As Lincoln faced the journey back to Springfield, he was a discouraged man. The Whig Party, splintered over slavery, was beginning to disintegrate, and as noted earlier, Lincoln's opposition to the war with Mexico had made him unpopular. It looked as if his political career had ended.

★ 3 ★

A CRIMINAL BETRAYAL

In Lincoln's day, Springfield, Illinois, was a bleak place.
There were some brick buildings in the city, but most of its houses were wood-frame structures or log cabins. Swaybacked horses stood submissively at hitching posts in front of markets, dry-goods stores, blacksmith shops, and saloons. John Hay, who studied law in Springfield and would become one of Lincoln's secretaries, described the place as "combining the meanness of the North with the barbarism of the South."

Lincoln took a kinder view of his hometown. He welcomed its familiar sights and sounds, but, disheartened as he was, he took little comfort from the gentle rains, the wildflowers in the fields, or the greening of the maples and the elms that stood along the avenues. He joked and laughed with old acquaintances, but a friend remembered that sometimes when the tall and often awkward man walked the streets, "depression hung on him, like a loose and dusty garment."

No sooner had Lincoln left Washington than he turned down an offer to become the governor of the Oregon Territory—a post he was sure would have no future. Chicago lawyer Grant Goodrich, a prosperous gentleman who wore

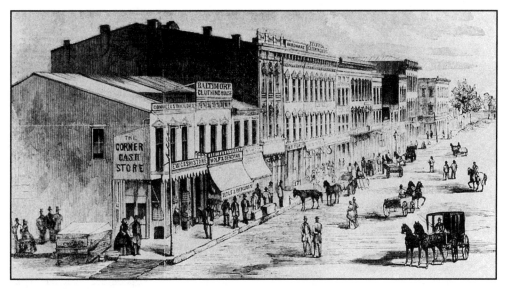

Springfield as it was in Lincoln's day. Lincoln's secretary John Hay, who knew the city well, wrote about "the dreary wastes of Springfield—a city combining the meanness of the North with the barbarism of the South." Lincoln took a kinder view of his hometown. In *Frank Leslie's Magazine*, December 22, 1860. *The collection of the author*

carefully tailored clothes, asked him to become a partner in his firm, but Lincoln shied away from practice in Chicago.

With rumpled hair and trousers much too short for his long legs, he returned to his long established partnership with Herndon, who was nine years younger than he was. Herndon was thin-lipped, black-eyed, and passionate. He and Mary Lincoln loathed each other, but Lincoln liked and trusted him and called him "Billy."

In the spring of 1849, John D. Johnston—son of Lincoln's stepmother—wrote to Lincoln, asking him to come at once to his father's farm in Coles County. Lincoln's father, Johnston said, was dying. Johnston wrote, "He Craves to See you all the time and he wonts you to Come if you are able to git hure, for you are his only Child that is of his own flush and blood. . . ."

Lincoln made the three-day journey only to discover that his father was recovering. Later, his stepbrother told him once again that his father was about to die, but this time Lincoln, who was especially busy at the time and thought

The Lincoln & Herndon law office. Its north windows gave the partners a clear view of the public square and the State Capitol. In *Frank Leslie's Magazine*, December 22, 1860. *The collection of the author*

that this might be another false alarm, didn't go. His father died without seeing his son again.

Lincoln and Herndon had a lot of friends in Illinois, and they soon rebuilt their practice. They shared a dingy office in the Tinsley Building, four blocks or so from Lincoln's house and across from the state capitol. Five years before, Herndon had spent $168.65 for a few necessities. "The furniture, somewhat dilapidated, consisted of one small desk and a table, a sofa . . . with raised head at one end, and half a dozen plain wooden chairs." To this collection, Herndon added one more table and a larger desk—equipped with pigeonholes— and a bookcase.

Herndon was almost as disorganized as Lincoln, and their office was a shambles. As they worked, they stacked their papers helter-skelter on the tables, on the desks, and in the dusty corners of the room; and when Lincoln left the office, he filed current documents behind the sweatband of his stovepipe hat.

Lincoln often wasted time. Herndon wrote, "Sometimes Lincoln would read something in the papers and that would suggest to him an idea and he would say, 'That puts me in mind of a story I heard down in Egypt in Illinois,' and then he would tell the story, and that story would suggest another, and so on. Nothing was done that morning."

The two men were opposites. Though Lincoln hated slavery, he believed that abolitionists often did more harm than good. He thought that their actions, if carried to extremes, would "shiver into fragments the Union of these States, tear to tatters its now venerated Constitution."

Breathlessly, Herndon took up one cause, then another, but he was a consistent abolitionist. He sent away for copies of the speeches of some of the leading abolitionists, and corresponded with the fiery Massachusetts preacher Theodore Parker, who said, "The man who attacks me to reduce me to slavery, in that moment of attack alienates his right to life, and if I were the fugitive, and could escape in no other way, I would kill him with as little compunction as I would drive a mosquito from my face."

Herndon was a fast, impatient reader, while his partner read deliberately, looking up from time to time, often frowning thoughtfully. Herndon, who wore expensive clothes and bright patent-leather shoes, nonetheless saw himself as a backwoods philosopher whose "mud instincts" told him what to do. He made decisions quickly. Lincoln spent long hours staring into space before deciding what to do. Herndon, who admired the New England intellectuals—the poets, novelists, and essayists—urged his partner to read novels and books on religion and philosophy, but

William Henry Herndon as he looked in middle age. Loyal as he always was to Lincoln, he disliked Lincoln's wife and found his sons unbearable. *Courtesy Lincoln Home National Historic Park*

Lincoln had no patience with romance, blind faith, or speculation and ignored these offerings. To keep up with politics and law, he read newspapers and law books. He was in love with language and read, often aloud, Shakespeare's plays and sonnets, the poetry of Robert Burns, and the King James Version of the Bible.

While Herndon worked in the office in Springfield, Lincoln rode the circuit. He took buggy rides or rode horseback from one of the fourteen county seats to another, most of them within the boundaries of the Eighth Judicial Circuit. Now and then, he practiced in Coles County, where his stepmother and stepbrother lived. On the circuit, he represented a variety of clients, including thieves and murderers. The system was much less tightly structured than it is now, and he sometimes acted as a judge.

Most county seats were windswept prairie towns, where the judges and lawyers stayed in the shabbiest of boardinghouses, eating food fried in lard and, on cold nights, sleeping two or three men in a bed.

Lincoln loved his wife and sons, but he liked the freedom of the road. On the circuit, he met men who recognized his genius and were later to help him when he reentered politics. One of these was Judge David Davis, a huge, good-natured man who was later to become an associate justice of the United States Supreme Court. Davis found Lincoln's company so stimulating that he missed him when he didn't show up at a meal.

Before he went to Washington to serve in Congress, Lincoln was involved in two cases in which slavery was an issue. The first was *Bailey v. Cromwell,* tried and appealed in 1841. Bailey claimed that he had purchased Nance, a young black servant, from Cromwell. Instead of cash, Bailey had given Cromwell an I.O.U. When the time came to pay for Nance, Bailey refused to pay, saying that he had not been given papers proving ownership and that Nance in effect had run away.

In circuit court, where Lincoln lost, and then in the Illinois Supreme Court, Lincoln represented Bailey. He won the case in the Illinois Supreme Court, arguing that while Nance was supposed to be a slave, she had been paid

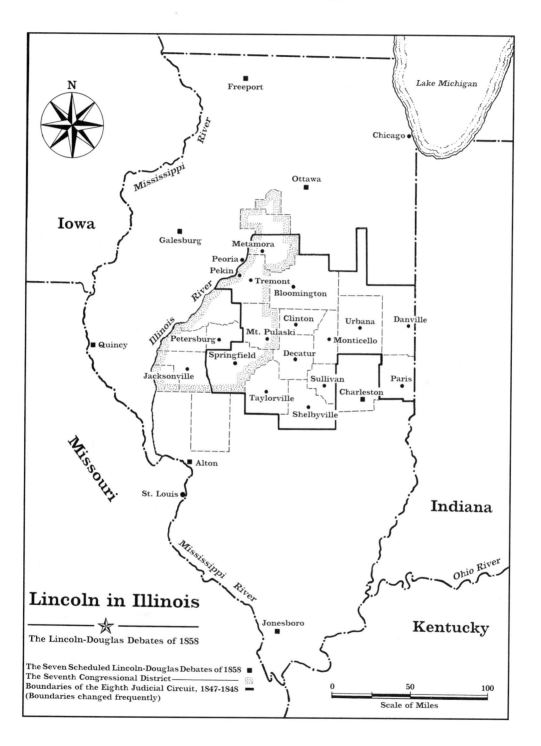

N

Lake Michigan

Freeport

Chicago

Iowa

Ottawa

Galesburg

Metamora

Mississippi River

Peoria

Pekin

Tremont

Bloomington

Clinton

Urbana

Danville

Illinois River

Quincy

Petersburg

Mt. Pulaski

Monticello

Springfield

Decatur

Jacksonville

Sullivan

Paris

Taylorville

Charleston

Shelbyville

Missouri

Alton

St. Louis

Indiana

Mississippi River

Ohio River

Lincoln in Illinois

★

The Lincoln-Douglas Debates of 1858

The Seven Scheduled Lincoln-Douglas Debates of 1858 ■
The Seventh Congressional District ⸺
Boundaries of the Eighth Judicial Circuit, 1847-1848 ▬
(Boundaries changed frequently)

Jonesboro

Kentucky

0   50   100

Scale of Miles

by Bailey and by other people and had been trusted and been given credit at stores in her neighborhood. Once he had established her good character and her clear residence in Illinois, Lincoln pointed out that Illinois was a free state. The court ruled that, in Illinois, every person was free without regard to color and that "the sale of a free person is illegal." Nance was declared forever free.

Six weeks after Lincoln died, Herndon—ever loyal to his partner and afraid that legend would obscure the man—urged his countrymen not to forget that Lincoln was "not a God—was a man: he was not perfect—had some defects & a few positive faults [but] he was a good man—an honest man." Lincoln demonstrated many times that he was an empathetic person—capable of deep affection, capable of imagining and feeling the distress of other people—but he made inexplicable mistakes. One of these was representing slaveholder Robert Matson.

The story of the Matson case is important for three reasons. First, it illustrates the tragedy of slavery. Second, it reveals a tendency in Lincoln to be indecisive. Third, it demonstrates the foolishness of his hope that colonization—the emigration of black people to West Africa, the Caribbean, or South America—might serve as a solution to his nation's racial problems.

Lincoln, who is often thought of as the greatest president in U.S. history, was a complicated man—aside from Thomas Jefferson, perhaps the most complicated man to serve as president. Most of his biographers, wanting to protect him, have ignored or given short shrift to the Matson case. Some have apologized for Lincoln, saying that he made only a halfhearted effort on behalf of his client. Nothing could be further from the truth. Lincoln always fought to win.

Robert Matson owned land in Kentucky and in Illinois. It was legal for slaveholders to take slaves to the free state of Illinois as long as they didn't keep them there. Every spring, Matson took a coffle of his slaves across the Ohio River, into Illinois, to work his fields. After they had brought his harvest in, he returned them to Kentucky.

Matson's trouble started in the fall of 1845, when he kept a slave named Jane in Illinois. Most slaves were given no surnames and were not allowed to marry, but Jane was married to Anthony Bryant, a freed slave who was one of Matson's overseers. Jane spent two years on Matson's farm in Illinois, with her husband and four children. Her happiness came to an end in 1847 when she had an argument with Matson's white housekeeper, who was also Matson's lover. Taking his housekeeper's part, Matson threatened to return Jane and her children to Kentucky, to be sold.

Panic-stricken, Bryant went to nearby Oakland, to enlist the help of Hiram Rutherford, a young doctor born and raised in Pennsylvania. Rutherford and innkeeper Gideon Ashmore promised to do what they could for him. After dark, Bryant took his wife and children to Oakland, where Ashmore hid them in an upstairs room, then waited anxiously to see what would happen next.

Matson hired lawyer Usher F. Linder—a heavy drinker and smooth talker, with proslavery sympathies—who saw to it that the runaways were found and taken into custody. Jane and her children were incarcerated in a Charleston jail. Most townspeople were in sympathy with Bryant and his wife and children, and some of them mounted an armed guard around the prison to intimidate a wagonload of Matson's henchmen who were hoping to kidnap the fugitives.

Lincoln was in Charleston as the Matson case took shape. In fact, he had been involved in two other cases there—in one of which he had been opposed by Linder. Admiring Lincoln, Linder asked him to be his co-counsel in the Matson case.

Lincoln must have had excruciating doubts about representing a slave owner. It was one thing to defend a murderer, to save someone from the gallows; it was quite another to send a young mother and her children into slavery. But, for reasons nobody has been able to explain, Lincoln said that he would work with Linder. Then, when Rutherford asked Lincoln to defend the Bryants, he refused. Lincoln later hinted that he might indeed switch sides, but, by that time, Rutherford was tired of Lincoln's indecision and had taken on another lawyer.

The trial was held on Saturday, October 16, 1847, in the evening. The brick courthouse, in the middle of the village green, was full of people. Against all the evidence—some of which Lincoln might have failed to study—he argued that Matson had never intended to keep Jane in Illinois. The court ruled against his argument. In language that was unmistakable, the presiding judge proclaimed that the Bryants should "be and remain free and discharged from all servitude to any person or persons from henceforth and forever."

Lincoln, in his heart of hearts, must have celebrated the release of Jane and her children. But by the time he represented Matson, he had won a seat in Congress and was soon to go to Washington. He probably never heard about what happened to the Bryants.

Following their liberation, Bryant and his wife decided they would colonize. They planned to move to Liberia, where they thought that they would be associated with a people sympathetic to them. Since slaves were kept in ignorance, it wasn't likely that the Bryants knew that most slaves in America had come from the valley and the delta of the Niger—a thousand miles east of Liberia and a region that itself had many languages and cultures. They probably didn't know that there were differences, in appearance and in language, among all the peoples of a continent that stretched five thousand miles from the Atlas Mountains in the north to the southern reaches of the South Atlantic. In their rush to escape from injustice in America, it never crossed their minds that Liberians would fail to welcome them with open arms.

Ashmore took them on a tour of Illinois to raise money for their journey. Antislavery folk in Charleston and in Springfield—including Herndon—were especially generous, and hoping for a happy life in a new home, the Bryants left for Africa. Later, a black Baptist minister went to Liberia to visit them and discovered that they had been scorned and cheated by Liberians and were living in deplorable conditions.

It must be said that Lincoln never recommended forced repatriation of black people; but, in his ignorance of the aspirations of most black Americans, he clung, sometimes desperately, to the notion that large numbers of them would go willingly to other places when in fact few of them would choose to leave America. His ignorance stemmed from his lack of association with black people. There were fewer than two hundred free black people in Springfield, most of whom were laborers or servants. In the whole state, there were few, if any, black citizens who felt free to talk to their white neighbors about more than changes in the weather.

In Springfield, Lincoln's only close black friend was his barber, William de Fleurville, called "Billy." Born in Haiti and having lived and learned his trade in Baltimore, Maryland, Fleurville had turned up broke in New Salem in the fall of 1831. It was there that Lincoln met him and befriended him. Fleurville stayed in New Salem long enough to save a little money and move on to Springfield, where he established the first barbershop in the town that would become the capital of Illinois in 1839. He was almost universally admired for his skill, generosity, and wit, and by the time Lincoln set up a law practice in Springfield, he had become a pillar of the black community.

While Fleurville struggled with Lincoln's wiry and unruly hair, Lincoln

The Lincoln house in Springfield, Illinois. This was where Lincoln and his family lived when he was elected president. At first, it was a single-story dwelling. As he prospered, he improved the property. Known as the "Lincoln Home," it is now a monument. *Williams College Sawyer Library*

gave him legal counsel. Lincoln was so fond of him that, even after he became president of the United States, he sorted out his legal problems for him. But no black person in Springfield, including Fleurville, would have talked to Lincoln about slavery or the segregation of the races. Certainly, Mary Lincoln's laundress—the dignified and beautiful Mariah Vance—would have been reluctant to do so.

It is pleasant to be able to report that, in 1864, Fleurville wrote to Lincoln, expressing deep affection for him and voicing his hope that he would be re-elected president so that "the oppressed will shout the name of their deliverer, and generations to come will rise up and call you blessed."

If Lincoln had a guilty conscience over Bryant and his family, he partially atoned for his involvement in their case when, with Herndon's help, he saved a young black man from a life of servitude. Soon after he returned from Washington, in the spring of 1849, Lincoln learned from a colleague that John Shelby, a free black youth from Illinois who lived with his mother, had been jailed in New Orleans. Shelby, working as a busboy and a deckhand on a Mississippi riverboat, had gone ashore without a pass. He hadn't known that in New Orleans all black people must not only carry papers that identified them, but were required to be indoors after dark. He had violated the curfew and was taken into custody.

Shelby couldn't pay his fine, and it looked as if he might be sold. Lincoln, tortured by the thought of a free person being enslaved, sent money to New Orleans to pay Shelby's fine and paid his passage back to Illinois. Herndon wrote that his and Lincoln's actions "restored the prisoner to his overjoyed mother."

Lincoln's son Edward died of tuberculosis on February 1, 1850. Mary Lincoln found it impossible to come to terms with her son's death. In solitude, Lincoln wept for his lost son but, in public, said no more than that he missed the boy.

Lincoln soon became one of the most skillful lawyers in his state. A colleague, who had heard him try at least a hundred cases, said of him, "Mr. Lincoln had a genius for seeing the real point in a case at once, and aiming steadily at it from the beginning of a trial to the end."

In jury trials, he had a habit of conceding minor points, nodding, smiling, then relentlessly repeating central arguments, so the jury would remember them.

Not long after Lincoln had left Washington, his hero Henry Clay—often called the "Great Pacificator" because he had written the Missouri Compromise of 1820–1821—started crafting what he hoped would become a lasting compromise, a series of resolutions that he believed would enable North and South to live peaceably with each other. Clay's Compromise of 1850

Henry Clay as he looked as an older man. When Clay died in 1852, Lincoln hoped that he might follow in Clay's political footsteps, but fate had greater things in store for him. *Williams College Sawyer Library*

admitted California to the Union as a free state. It provided that the people of New Mexico and Utah determine, in elections, whether their states would be slave or free. It also gave slaveholders a strict fugitive slave law, providing for the return of runaways to their masters—an extension of the Fugitive Slave Act of 1793, which had made it a criminal offense to give aid and comfort to a runaway.

Since Lincoln's childhood, legislators had been playing a game with slavery. As one state, then another, was admitted to the Union, they had repeatedly redressed the balances, admitting a slave state at the same time as a free state, but because of the wording of the Constitution, slave states dominated Congress.

Abolitionists were bitterly opposed to compromise. A leading abolitionist, James Forten, who was born and raised in Philadelphia, Pennsylvania, fairly trumpeted his anger over the extension of the Fugitive Slave Act of 1793.

The United States in 1854

Slave States and Territories, 1821 ⎯⎯⎯⎯⎯⎯⎯
Admitted as Slave State, 1845 ⎯⎯⎯⎯⎯⎯⎯
Opened to Slavery by the Compromise of 1850 ⎯⎯⎯⎯
Opened to Slavery by the Kansas-Nebraska Act, 1854 ⎯⎯
(Boundaries as of 1854)

0   200   400
Scale of Miles

Forten was one of many free black Americans who had fought against the British in the Revolutionary War. He was a drummer and a powder boy—an assistant gunner—aboard the privateer *Royal Louis* sailing in the service of the patriots. After the *Royal Louis* was captured by the British, Forten spent seven months as prisoner number 4102, in the hold of a British prison ship.

As a young man who had served his country and had every reason to be bitter over laws protecting interests of slaveholders, he wrote, "The dog is protected and pampered at the board of his master, while the poor African and his descendent . . . is branded with infamy." He said that there would soon be laws authorizing the police to capture any black man "who dares to walk the streets without a collar on his neck!"

In later life, Forten was a sailmaker. He prospered and, until his death in 1842, was a dedicated abolitionist, giving both time and money to the cause.

Lincoln, who clung to the notion that, under the Constitution, slaveholders had the right to pursue and capture runaways, and believing that Clay's Compromise of 1850 might put an end to the trouble over slavery, was inclined to accept it. He did suggest, however, that the law be modified to reduce the possibility that free black people would be kidnapped and sold into slavery.

Lincoln kept a low profile, but he was heard from now and then, and he campaigned successfully for his thirty-seven-year-old friend Richard Yates, who first took a seat in the U.S. Congress in 1851. After serving as a congressman, Yates became the wartime governor of Illinois, where he recruited loyal young men for the Union Army and restrained the state's powerful Confederate elements, most of which were in the southern portions of the state—parts sharing borders with Missouri and Kentucky.

Henry Clay died in 1852. At first, Lincoln hoped that he might follow in Clay's footsteps and perhaps resuscitate his party, but fate had better things in store for him.

In 1853, as spring brought to life the vast prairies that surrounded Springfield, Mary gave birth to another son, Thomas, named for Lincoln's father. As he grew up, Thomas—called "Tad"—and his older brother Willie drove Herndon to distraction.

> Sometimes Lincoln would, when his wife had gone to church or kicked him out of the house, bring to the office Willie and Tad. . . . These children would take down the books, empty the ash buckets, coal ashes, inkstand, papers, gold pens, letters, etc., etc., in a pile and then dance on the pile. Lincoln would say nothing, so abstracted was he and so blinded to his children's faults.

On January 4, 1854, Senator Stephen Douglas—who, as a lawyer, had locked horns with Lincoln many times—took a step that upset Lincoln so profoundly that it forced him to return to politics.

Douglas was, in some ways, a generous man but was blind where black people were concerned. Unlike Lincoln, he saw no contradiction between slavery and democracy. As chairman of the Committee on Territories, which controlled the destiny of vast, undeveloped Western regions, he was faced with the task of establishing a government for the territories of Kansas and Nebraska. In constructing such a government, he introduced the Kansas-Nebraska Act, which would sweep away the Compromise of 1850 and replace it with a measure that would give the settlers themselves the power to determine whether to be slave or free. In short, it would promote the spread of slavery. Douglas, sugarcoating it, said that it would do no more than give settlers what he called "popular sovereignty."

For four months, against violent opposition from both radical and conservative antislavery legislators, Douglas—who by then was extremely powerful—worked to clear the way for passage of his legislation. He threatened, argued with, and bullied fellow legislators, until in May his bill was voted on and passed.

Lincoln said that passage of the measure "took us by surprise—astounded us. . . . We were thunderstruck and stunned."

Douglas had given in to proslavery sentiments in order to promote his chances of becoming president. Senator Salmon P. Chase—later to become Lincoln's secretary of the Treasury—had been none too happy with the Fugitive Slave Act of 1850 but was outraged by the Kansas-Nebraska Act, which he called "a gross violation of a sacred pledge, a criminal betrayal."

Lincoln was slow to speak, slow to act, but he thought almost constantly about the implications of what he called the Nebraska Act. Herndon said that he spent hours brooding over what he saw as fatal flaws in Douglas's reasoning. If, for example, it was wrong to import slaves into the United States, it must be wrong to import them into a free territory. It was wrong to let a scattering of people in a thinly populated territory make a decision that would echo through the ages, a decision that might save or destroy American democracy. Lincoln knew that it was time to fight.

★ 4 ★

A UNIVERSAL FEELING

Lincoln gave his first important speech on slavery in Springfield, in the fall of 1854, when the Illinois State Fair was in progress.

Families had come to the state capital in wagons and dilapidated buggies, come with their prize animals and with wagonloads of produce. Preachers had come and people selling patent medicines. There were exhibitions of milk cows and bulls and breeding sows. Sheep were judged for the softness of their fleece and rams for the glory of their horns. There was to be a speech by Stephen Douglas, who was by then so powerful that people called him "Little Giant." Lincoln planned to be on hand to answer Douglas.

The contrasts between Lincoln and the senator were disconcerting, almost comical. Lincoln, who was six feet four, was nearly a foot taller than his adversary. He was thin. His skin was dark and leathery. Sometimes, as he began to speak, his voice was high. He was gentle. Douglas, on the other hand, was dynamic and commanding, often fierce. His cheeks were pink. His thick brown hair was long enough to conceal a sturdy neck. His heavy brows sheltered bright and penetrating eyes. His voice was deep.

The contest between the two had already lasted many years and was destined to continue until 1860, when Lincoln was to be elected president. They met first in 1834, when both were in their twenties and both were serving in the Illinois state legislature. As young lawyers on the circuit, they had opposed each other many times, once in a case concerning theft by a farmer of another farmer's pigs. In 1843, Douglas won a seat in Congress, went to live in Washington, and returned to Illinois only to campaign for reelection.

The superficial differences between the men were no more dramatic than the temperamental ones. At home, Lincoln sometimes lost his temper, but he was fully in control of his emotions in court or in debate. He told jokes and frontier stories. Though he often used sarcasm as a weapon, he was thought of as a gentleman. Douglas, born in Vermont, went west when he was young and adopted western ways. He seldom talked about his boyhood. He told no funny stories. John Quincy Adams wrote about the young man's manner as he pressed a point in Congress: "His face was convulsed, his gesticulation frantic. . . . In the midst of his roaring, to save himself choking, he stripped off and cast away his cravat, and unbuttoned his waistcoat and had the air and aspect of a half-naked pugilist."

What mattered most were moral contrasts—differences between their views of right and wrong. Lincoln knew that black people loved at least as deeply as he did. Their fears were his, their pain his own. Douglas lacked Lincoln's broad humanity. Where black people were concerned, he was cold, sometimes vicious. He wasn't joking when he said that he preferred a white man to a black man and a black man to a crocodile. He was loyal to the Union, but he felt no moral outrage over slavery.

Here were two men who were polar opposites. Both lacked wide acquaintance with black people but, if Lincoln harbored prejudice growing out of ignorance, Douglas was encumbered by a pinched and crippled view of all humanity.

By 1854, when Lincoln—fired by a vision of democracy in peril—went back into politics, Douglas was no longer casting off his necktie and frantically unbuttoning his vest, but his deep voice and the fierceness of his scowl had more power to command an audience than it had had when he was young. He was a seasoned politician, but, in the fall of 1854, he was suffering from a self-inflicted wound. The storm over passage of the Kansas-Nebraska Act had swept into Illinois. Douglas said that he could go from Boston to Chicago by the light of his own burning effigies. Abolitionists spoke against him, as did Whigs and many of his fellow Democrats. An editorial in a paper called *Free West* voiced an outrage felt by many citizens: "The free people of Illinois thus have the mortification of seeing one of their Senators acting as the tool of Southern slave-drivers."

Not long before he confronted Lincoln at the State Fair, Douglas had stood on a hastily constructed platform in Chicago's Public Square and faced the groans and hisses of a hostile audience. The night was hot, and in tenements around the square, women in spare cotton dresses and men in their undershirts leaned on their windowsills. In the crowd were recent immigrants from Ireland, Germany, and Sweden. Gangs of thugs, some armed with knives and pistols, most of them driven by the fear that slavery would become universal and put them in competition with slave labor, kept the crowd in an uproar. Against the tumult, Douglas boomed out a defense of the Kansas-Nebraska Act. He braved the storm until midnight, when at last he shouted, "Abolitionists of Chicago! It is now Sunday morning. I will go to church and you may go to hell!"

Douglas, haunted by the trouble in Chicago, turned down an offer to face Lincoln in debate in Springfield, saying, "This is my meeting. The people came here to hear me, and I want to talk to them."

He was scheduled to speak on Tuesday, October 3. Five thousand seats had been set up in an outdoor amphitheater, but it rained and his listeners took refuge in the hall of the House of Representatives. The air in the chamber was both hot and humid. Many people had to stand or sit together in the aisles.

As Douglas spoke, Lincoln listened in the lobby. He was like a man possessed—pacing, gesturing, and frowning.

Douglas painted a heroic picture of the settlement of western territories, of the hardships borne by pioneers who had crossed the mountains and the deserts. He talked about their right to decide important questions for them-

Chicago, Illinois in 1845. *Prints and photographs division, Library of Congress*

selves—"popular sovereignty." He talked about the ineffectiveness of Clay's Missouri Compromise of 1820–1821 and the shortcomings of the Compromise of 1850, which he himself had shepherded through Congress. He praised his latest compromise. He scorned Lincoln's fear that, if legislation failed to outlaw slavery, slavery would accompany or follow after settlement. He said that slavery only flourished in mild climates, that it couldn't be imported into northern territories, into regions where cruel winter storms swept across the hills and mountains.

When Douglas finished, Lincoln stood on a stairway and announced that he would answer him the next day. As Lincoln spoke to a crowd at least as large as the one that had gathered on the day before, he stood sweating in his shirtsleeves. When he pointed out the flaws in his opponent's arguments, people in the crowd expressed approval. He was interrupted often by applause.

Douglas sat in the front row and exchanged a few remarks with Lincoln. Herndon, who was listening and watching, wrote that Lincoln faced his audience directly, his legs straight, his toes pointing forward. Lincoln's voice, high at first, soon became "melodious and musical." Sometimes he emphasized important points with his right hand but more often with a motion of his head.

Lincoln's speech, as it was delivered on October 4, in Springfield, was not recorded. He gave essentially the same speech twelve days later, in Peoria, where reporters wrote it down. Lincoln covered much familiar territory, emphasized his loyalty to his country and his devotion to the Union. He argued that the founding fathers knew that slavery, if permitted to survive, would undermine democracy. He pointed out that slavery had often taken root in states and territories where it had been neither outlawed nor approved. He argued for the restoration of the Missouri Compromise of 1820–1821.

He had said these things before, but now his audience—described as "attentive" and "intelligent"—saw something new in Lincoln. He was sounding almost like an abolitionist. He was leaving little room for doubt about how much he hated slavery.

> I hate it because of the monstrous injustice of slavery itself. I hate it because it . . . enables the enemies of free institutions with plausability to taunt us as hypocrites, causes the real friends of freedom to doubt our sincerity, and especially because it forces so many good men among ourselves into an open war with the very fundamental principles of civil liberty, criticizing the Declaration of Independence, and insisting that there is no right principle of action but self-interest.

Using a review of laws governing the trade in captured Africans—Africans often captured by their fellow Africans—as an argument against the spread of slavery, he pointed out that, from the first, senators and congressmen took a hostile view of the slave trade.

> In 1794 they prohibited an outgoing slave-trade—that is, the taking of slaves from the United States to sell. In 1798 they prohibited the bringing of slaves from Africa into the Mississippi Territory, this Territory then comprising what are now the states of Mississippi and Alabama. . . . In 1800, they prohibited American citizens from trading in slaves between foreign countries . . . for instance, from Africa to Brazil.

The expulsion of abolitionists from Boston's Tremont Temple in 1860. Racial outbursts like this one were commonplace throughout the North before and during Lincoln's time. *Harper's Weekly*, December 15, 1860. *Williams College Sawyer Library*

Lincoln said that, in 1807, they levied heavy fines on Americans caught engaging in the African slave trade; and in 1820—finding these laws ineffective—they declared that men found participating in the slave trade were engaged in piracy and should be executed.

Lincoln chided his opponent for calling the Kansas-Nebraska Act a "sacred" document. Using heavy sarcasm, he said that Douglas sent the slaveholder on his way, telling him, "Go, and God speed you." He said that, if Douglas had his way, slavery would become "the chief jewel of the nation—the very figurehead of the ship of state."

Lincoln told his listeners that a supporter of the recent compromise had called the Declaration of Independence a "self-evident lie." Lincoln said, "In old Independence Hall seventy-eight years ago, the very doorkeeper would have throttled the man and thrust him into the street." He made a plea for unity: "Let North and South—let all Americans—let all lovers of liberty everywhere join in the great and good work. If we do this, we shall not only have saved the Union, but we shall have so saved it as to make and keep it forever worthy of the saving."

He pointed out that most white citizens were opposed to accepting freed slaves and free black Americans as their equals. "Whether this feeling accords with justice and sound judgment is not the sole question. . . . A universal feeling, whether well or ill founded, cannot be safely disregarded."

Indeed, in a democracy, a universal feeling must be recognized; but, as Lincoln later demonstrated, if that feeling goes against natural law, goes against the principles of that same democracy, an effort should be made to alter it. Following Lincoln's death, it would take more than one hundred years to make changes that would bring what black abolitionist Frederick Douglass called "the dawn of a new day."

In Lincoln's time, and long thereafter, immigrants were competing with black people for employment. There were black professionals—teachers, writers, publishers, printers, sailors, blacksmiths, harnessmakers, masons, cabinetmakers, undertakers, dentists, barbers—but most black men and women were unskilled and, therefore, a threat to unskilled white immigrants.

In the great cities of the North, racial tensions had brought on a rash of riots in which black people had been brutalized and killed. Unrest had been common not

William Lloyd Garrison, probably in his fifties. He was a nonviolent abolitionist who was physically courageous. He praised the Declaration of Independence, but he cursed the Constitution, calling it "a covenant with death and agreement with hell." *National Archives*

only in Chicago, but also in Boston, New York, and Philadelphia. Gatherings of abolitionists had been attacked. Nonviolent abolitionist William Lloyd Garrison—a small, balding man, who wore thick, wire-rimmed glasses—had been subject to brutality. On October 21, 1835, following his appearance at a meeting of the Boston Female Anti-Slavery Society, he was seized by racists and dragged into State Street, where his tormentors tore the shirt off his back, tied a rope around his waist, and led him across the cobblestones, taunting and insulting him. It was said that he kept his dignity and showed not a shred of fear.

In New York, in response to black antislavery agitation, white mobs had invaded theaters where black actors were performing. In 1822, a dozen white supremacists bought tickets to a performance at the African Grove Theater. They all but destroyed the place, stripped the costumes off the women, clubbed the proprietor. Also in New York, gangs of white men harassed one black congregation, then another and another. In 1829, two white sailors, egged on by a group of racists, entered the African Ebeneezer Church during Sunday services. They yelled and swore at the parishioners and picked a fight with one of them, a strong and determined man named Jacob Sands, who drove them off.

In 1834, in Philadelphia, several hundred immigrants—most of them from Germany and Ireland—armed with clubs, marched from Independence Hall into a black neighborhood. An onlooker wrote about the terror of that night: "They were joined by others, and all proceeded to places of amusement where many Negroes were congregated, on South Street." There, members of the mob proceeded to attack unarmed black men. The rioters knocked down flimsy houses occupied by black people of all ages—men, women, and their children. "In a three day uprising, thirty-one houses and two churches were destroyed and Stephen James, an honest, industrious colored man, was killed."

In 1838, also in Philadelphia, a mob burned Pennsylvania Hall—where abolitionists of both races gathered—and "burned the Shelter for Colored Orphans at Thirteenth and Callowhill streets."

Lincoln, having reasoned that a "universal feeling" cannot be disregarded, having recognized that trouble would accompany integration of the races, knew that dark days lay ahead, but he still hoped that compromise—other than the kind spelled out in the Kansas-Nebraska Act—might at least delay a crisis.

As the Illinois State Fair went forward, abolitionists—among them Elijah Lovejoy's brother, Owen—gathered in Springfield to organize opposition to the spread of slavery. Eventually, these men joined forces with William H. Seward, a senator from New York State, and other East Coast politicians to form an antislavery party. They called themselves "Republicans"—a name now used to describe a party that has changed dramatically since Lincoln's day. Having heard Lincoln's speech, the founders of the party asked him if he would join them; but Lincoln, wanting time to think about abandoning the Whigs, hitched his horse to his buggy and left town. He had business in Tremont, near Peoria, and this was as good a time as any to attend to it.

In the 1854 elections, Douglas suffered more than his opponents thought he would. Both he and his party faltered. Democrats fared badly in New England, Pennsylvania, Indiana, and Ohio. They lost ground in Illinois.

Lincoln had long had his eye on the Senate, and after Douglas's decline, he wrote letters to his friends, asking them to test the weight of support for him. However, in 1855, he failed to win the nomination and went back to his law practice.

He and Herndon represented several railroads: the Illinois Central, the Ohio & Mississippi, and the Rock Island line. Because of his awkwardness and country ways, he was ignored or treated coldly by most successful lawyers in Chicago and was scorned by many of their colleagues from Baltimore, Philadelphia, Pittsburgh, and New York. Especially rude to him was Edwin M. Stanton, a wily Pittsburgh lawyer who would later serve as Lincoln's secretary of war. In forgiving and sometimes defending Stanton, Lincoln demonstrated one of his endearing qualities. His readiness to forgive men who had slighted him stemmed from his belief that it was a waste of time and energy to hold a grudge or seek revenge.

At last, in 1856, Lincoln saw that he could use his powers of persuasion to forge an alliance between radicals both black and white—called "Black Republicans"—and the more conservative antislavery members of the party. He joined forces with Republicans as they campaigned against the spread of slavery.

It was none too soon for Lincoln to give his allegiance to a party representing his convictions. More and more Americans were protesting against slavery—called by abolitionists that "peculiar institution." In the spring of the same year that the Kansas-Nebraska Act was voted into law, a young man was arrested in Boston, Massachusetts, and was returned to slavery in Alexandria, Virginia.

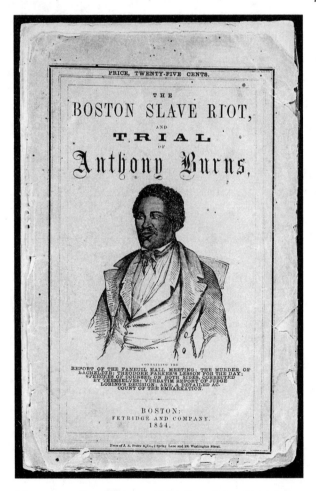

PRICE, TWENTY-FIVE CENTS.

THE
BOSTON SLAVE RIOT,
AND
TRIAL
OF
Anthony Burns,

BOSTON:
FETRIDGE AND COMPANY.
1854.

The cover of an 1854 pamphlet describing the trial of Anthony Burns, a fugitive from slavery.
Williams College Chapin Library

Anthony Burns was one of many fugitives arrrested in the North, but his case attracted wide attention. On March 25, 1854, he was leased out as a stevedore. After working a full day, he fell asleep in a secluded corner of a ship that then left port, sailed down Chesapeake Bay, and took him out to sea. He had not intended to escape, but when the ship docked in Boston, he found work and settled down in a black neighborhood on a slope of Beacon Hill. Soon, he grew homesick for his people in Virginia. Burns was one of those few slaves who had learned to read and write, and he wrote to his brother, arranging to have his letter postmarked in a town in Canada. His master, Charles F. Suttle, somehow guessed that Burns was in Boston, not in Canada, and had him arrested.

Under the provisions of all fugitive slave acts, it was illegal to help runaways; but New England abolitionists had never cringed in the face of unjust laws, and they went to work for Burns, who was imprisoned in Boston's Old Courthouse—a large, impressive building with barred windows.

On March 26, outraged abolitionists gathered in Fanueil Hall—a scene of revolutionary gatherings and referred to as "the cradle of liberty." There, Theodore Parker, who had bright blue eyes and large, expressive hands, spoke to a gathering of angry men and women, including free black citizens. Led by Thomas Wentworth Higginson, who was later to command a regiment of liberated slaves, the protesters marched to the Old Courthouse. Using a heavy beam, they battered down one of the doors, and as they entered a hallway, one of them stabbed a marshal, killing him. The attackers failed to free the prisoner and retreated. The murderer, probably protected by his friends, was never found.

Charlotte Forten, a black student living in nearby Salem, went to Boston while Burns was imprisoned there.

> Everything was quieter—outwardly—than we expected, but still much real indignation and excitement prevail. We walked past the courthouse which is now lawlessly converted into a prison, and filled with soldiers, some of whom were looking from the windows, with an air of insolent authority, which made my blood boil, while I felt the strongest contempt for their cowardice and servility.

That evening, Forten and a friend of hers dined with Garrison and his wife, Helen Benson. At supper, Garrison spoke against Higginson's violent tactics, and Forten, who all but worshiped Garrison, watched him as he spoke "beautifully of the non-resistant principles to which he has kept firm." But she did not agree with him. She wrote that, in resisting tyrants, she would "fight for liberty until death."

Charlotte Forten. At 25, when she was teaching children of freed slaves, a young Union officer called her "the belle of the Sea Islands." She was always disciplined and serious. *Moorland-Spingarn Research Center, Howard University*

Because Burns was a slave, he was denied a trial and, at a hearing, was declared a fugitive. As Burns was taken to the waterfront to be returned to slavery, the city fathers took no chances. Burns was surrounded by eight companies of artillery, a regiment of cavalry, and a regiment of infantry. Forten wrote, "Oh! With what deep sorrow do we think of what will doubtless be the fate of that poor man, when he is again consigned to the horrors of slavery."

Burns was kept in irons and imprisoned in Virginia until a committee of Bostonians paid for his freedom. He returned to Boston, where he lectured against slavery and became a minister. Weakened by imprisonment, he died when he was only twenty-eight.

In the spring of 1856, violence erupted on the floor of the U.S. Senate, after Massachusetts Senator Charles Sumner criticized South Carolina Senator Andrew Pickens Butler. Sumner, an aggressive abolitionist, was a hero to his colleagues. He was a handsome man with a head of thick dark hair, flashing eyes, and a strong chin. He was fond of fancy clothes and wore purple flowered vests.

In a speech, started on May 22 and concluded on May 23, he stated flatly that Butler was disloyal to the Union. Sumner said, "The Senator dreams that he can subdue the North. . . . How little that Senator knows himself or the strength of the cause he persecutes! He is but mortal man; against him is an immortal principle. With finite power, he wrestles with the infinite, and he must fall. Against him are the invincible sentiments of the human heart; against him is God."

Butler wasn't in the Senate chamber during Sumner's long oration so did not respond to the attack, but two days later, Butler's nephew, Congressman Preston S. Brooks, approached the Massachusetts senator. The event that followed was reported in *The Liberator*, a weekly antislavery paper published by Garrison:

ATTEMPT TO MURDER HON. CHARLES SUMNER

Washington, May 22. Shortly before two o'clock this afternoon, the Senate having adjourned, Mr. Sumner was sitting in his place writing very busily. Preston Brooks, of S.C., approached him saying, "Mr. Sumner, I have read your speech twice. It is a libel on South Carolina, and on Mr. Butler, who is a relative of mine." Brooks struck him with a heavy cane, upon which Mr. Sumner sprung up from his seat to defend himself, with such violence that the heavy desk before him was wrenched from the floor. . . . He was, however, so much staggered as to be rendered powerless, and the blows were repeated until he was senseless. The two cuts upon his head are each about two inches in length and very deep.

Charles Sumner in his early days. Sumner was a senator and a persistent abolitionist. In 1856, in the Senate chamber, he was physically attacked by Representative Preston S. Brooks of South Carolina. *Williams College Sawyer Library*

Sumner, stunned and soaked in his own blood, was carried to an empty office. After he gained consciousness and was treated by a doctor, he was carried to his home, where it took him nearly three years to recover.

Also in 1856, John Charles Frémont—famous as a soldier and explorer—became the first Republican presidential candidate. The delegates to the National Republican Convention came close to voting Lincoln its first vice presidential candidate, but Lincoln lost the nomination. He went on to make effective speeches for the ticket, and Republicans fared well in Illinois. Nevertheless, Frémont lost the election to Democract James Buchanan.

On June 16, 1858, as the South drifted ever closer to rebellion, Lincoln was chosen, by acclaim, as "the first and only choice of the Republicans of Illinois for the United States Senate" to run against Stephen Douglas.

★ 5 ★

IN HIS PRISON HOUSE

In his speech accepting his party's nomination, Lincoln made a prophecy. In Springfield, on June 16, 1858, he quoted words that appear, in one form or another, three times in the New Testament, in Matthew, Mark, and Luke: "A house divided against itself cannot stand." He went on to say, "I believe this Government cannot endure permanently half slave and half free. I do not expect the Union to be dissolved—I do not expect the house to fall—but I do expect that it will cease to be divided."

Douglas, whose fortunes had improved since 1854, opened his campaign for reelection on July 9, in Chicago. He spoke from a balcony of an elegant hotel, the Tremont House. Attacking what came to be called Lincoln's "house divided speech," he said it was belligerent. The nation had been half slave and half free for more than fifty years. Why could it not continue as such?

The next day, in the same city and from the same balcony, Lincoln answered him. He said that he had only stated what he believed to be a universal truth. He said that the states would be divided only if slavery gained the upper hand.

Lincoln's perennial opponent Stephen Douglas at the time of his scheduled debates with Lincoln. They had met many times before in debate. *The National Archives*

He made a plea for unity: "Let us discard all this quibbling about . . . this race and the other race being inferior." He asked that his countrymen lay aside such arguments and "unite as one people throughout this land, until we shall once more stand up declaring that all men are created equal."

Lincoln was a worried man. Not only had the Kansas-Nebraska Act made the further spread of slavery likely, but the U.S. Supreme Court's Dred Scott decision—handed down six months before—had, in Lincoln's words, come close to making "slavery national throughout the United States."

Kicked around in lower courts in Missouri since 1846, the Dred Scott case had at last gone on appeal to the nation's highest court, where the justices had ruled five to four against Dred Scott, a former slave who had lived long enough in Wisconsin Territory—where slavery was illegal—to be freed. Writing the majority opinion, Chief Justice Roger B. Taney ruled that Scott must be returned to slavery. Taney said that the Missouri Compromise of 1820–1821 was unconstitutional. He said that the federal government had no right to outlaw slavery in the territories, and he added that, according to the Constitution, black people had "no rights that white people were bound to respect." The court had ruled, in effect, that black people were not, and never could become, full citizens. It followed, then, that Scott was not allowed to argue in a court of law. Case dismissed.

Lincoln's response to the Dred Scott decision came directly from the meditations of his heart. Speaking not just of Scott, but of each and every slave—man, woman, child—he said:

> All the powers of the earth seem rapidly combining against him. Mammon is after him; ambition follows, and philosophy follows, and the Theology of the day is fast joining the cry. They have him in his prison house; they have searched his person, and left no prying instrument with him. One after another, they have closed the heavy iron doors upon him, and now they have him, as it were, bolted in with a lock of a hundred keys, which can never be unlocked without the concurrence of every key; the keys in the hands of a hundred different men, and they scattered to a hundred different and distant places; and they stand musing as to what invention, in all the dominions of mind and matter, can be produced to make the impossibility of his escape more complete than it is.

It wasn't hard to understand why Lincoln thought that he was witnessing a conspiracy of slave power. He didn't trust President Buchanan, who was trying to mollify the South. Though Chief Justice Taney and four of his associates had turned the clock back almost forty years, Stephen Douglas praised the Dred Scott decision and expected it to stand. Lincoln reasoned that these men—representing the three branches of the government—must have communicated now and then and that, even if they hadn't, their moves might somehow have been coordinated. In fact, there was no conspiracy, but there was a rush of evidence that, in view of the Kansas-Nebraska Act and the Dred Scott decision, slavery might indeed overwhelm democracy.

Lincoln knew that careless threats and foolish actions might ignite a rebellion, but he was increasingly determined to arrest the spread of a disease that his country's most distinguished statesmen—from George Washington to Henry Clay—had identified as the greatest danger to democracy. He declared Taney's ruling in the Dred Scott case "a burlesque upon judicial decisions, and a slander and profanation upon the honored names and sacred history" of his nation. He said that the ruling must be overturned.

On July 24, 1858, Lincoln wrote a short note to Douglas. He said, in part,

> My dear sir: Will it be agreeable to you to make an arrangement for you and myself to divide time, and address the same audiences . . . ? Mr. Judd, who will hand you this, is authorized to receive your answer; and, if agreeable to you, to enter into the terms of such arrangement.
>
> Your obedient servant,
>
> A. Lincoln

Douglas and his challenger bargained over details, but this time, Douglas had no choice but to stand on the same platform with Lincoln. He told a friend, "I shall have my hands full. He is the strong man of his party—full of wit, facts, dates—and the best stump speaker, with his droll ways and dry jokes, in the West."

The two men were scheduled to meet in "joint discussions" in seven towns around the state: Ottawa, Freeport, Jonesboro, Charleston, Galesburg, Quincy, and Alton. As it turned out, the candidates campaigned in many other towns—in auditoriums, at county fairs, on street corners.

Lincoln sometimes traveled in his buggy. Now and then, he hired a carriage. Most times, he went by rail. Once, he and Douglas traveled on the same steamboat.

Douglas had a private railroad car, which was decked with bunting, flags, and banners and contained a perfectly appointed dining room and sleeping quarters to accommodate an impressive entourage—advisors, secretaries, bodyguards, and servants. His wife, Adele, who was clever and attractive, went with him and worked with him.

In the train was a brass cannon, mounted on a flatcar and attended by two gunners in blue uniforms. As the gunners fired the cannon to announce the senator's approach, the car lurched and almost jumped the tracks. Often, Lincoln found himself in the same train with Douglas, riding in an ordinary rail-car, where he worked on a speech or slept upright in his seat with his legs stretched out in the aisle. At times, he must have felt like a lean and hungry hound, nipping at the heels of the more distinguished Douglas.

The first debate, on August 21, at Ottawa, brought at least ten thousand strangers to the thriving steamboat port on the northern reaches of the Illinois River, which flowed southwest diagonally across the state until it joined the Mississippi River, at a bend above St. Louis. People came in riverboats and barges. Seventeen railroad cars brought two thousand people from Chicago. Other trains carried parties from La Salle and from Peru. A reporter for the New York *Evening Post* wrote that people "poured in, till Ottawa was one mass of active life. Men, women and children, old and young, the dwellers of the broad prairies, had turned their backs on the plough and had come to listen to the two champions of the two parties. Military companies were out; martial music sounded and salutes of artillery thundered in the air."

Lincoln, coming from Chicago, arrived in Ottawa at noon. His supporters joined him in a long parade—comprised of floats, military companies, and carriages bearing local dignitaries. They stopped at the Mansion House, then marched onward. Douglas and his party followed. In Lafayette Square, the debaters waited for unruly members of the crowd to settle down. At 2:30 P.M., the short, pugnacious Douglas and the tall, mild-mannered Lincoln shook hands, and the first debate began.

Douglas opened with a sharp attack on Lincoln. In a deep, insistent voice, he said that Lincoln and his fellow politicians had, since 1854, taken part in an effort to destroy the Whig Party and to divide and conquer Democrats. He quoted parts of what he called a "radical Republican platform," supposedly put together by Lincoln four years earlier in Springfield. Insisting on the right of every state and territory to determine its own policies, Douglas charged that Lincoln was in favor of imposing uniformity on all sections of the country.

His opening salvo was so ferocious that it unnerved Lincoln. As we have seen, Lincoln liked to think things through, labor over his responses. Uncomfortable, he hesitated, then became defensive. He said that he knew nothing of the drafting of the platform. Instead of speaking plainly, he used legal terms and legal arguments, but he made important points, points that would serve him well throughout the coming months. Again, he suggested a conspiracy to make slavery universal.

Douglas scoffed at Lincoln's belief in a conspiracy. He defended the Dred Scott decision, said that it should be honored by all law-abiding citizens.

Lincoln asked, "Then what is necessary for the nationalization of slavery?" Answering his own question, he said, "It is merely for the Supreme Court to decide that no State under the Constitution can exclude it."*

Lincoln quoted Clay, calling him his "beau ideal of a statesman—the man for whom I fought all my humble life."

> Henry Clay once said of a class of men who would repress all tendencies to liberty and ultimate emancipation, that they must, if they would do this, go back to the era of our independence, and muzzle the cannon which thundered its joyous return; they must penetrate the human soul, and eradicate there the love of liberty; and then, and not till then, could they perpetuate slavery in this country!

Lincoln said, as he had said before, that Taney's ruling must be overturned. Douglas had once been a judge in the Illinois Supreme Court, and in debate, Lincoln so referred to him. "But I cannot shake Judge Douglas's teeth loose from the Dred Scott decision."

When the first of the joint debates came to a close and the men stepped down from the high platform, Douglas's supporters picked him up and carried him to his hotel. Lincoln's people pushed and jostled him and, much against his will, bore him aloft. An unkind reporter wrote of how grotesque he looked, clutching at the heads of his supporters, his legs "dangling from their shoul-

---

*Lincoln knew that, even then, there were cases coming up before the Court that would make such a ruling possible.

ders, and his pantaloons pulled up so as to expose his underwear almost to his knees."

The next debate was held on August 27, in Freeport, an abolitionist stronghold, near the northern limits of the state, and a town served by the Galena & Chicago Union Railroad. Freeport was cold and damp. Douglas's brass cannon and the efforts of townspeople, on behalf of one candidate or the other, drew a smaller crowd than had attended the debate in Ottawa.

Though Henry Clay was Lincoln's "beau ideal" of a statesman, he was a slaveholder who believed that slavery should be eliminated slowly. He was, therefore, a constant compromiser. Abolitionists, both black and white, saw compromise as no more than an excuse for the continuance of slavery. This anonymous cartoon expresses bitterness toward the cruelty of compromise. The whipping is, of course, imaginary. *Massachusetts Historical Society*

Lincoln, having had almost a week to dig up facts and prepare his arguments, said that, in accusing him of having drafted the Republican platform, Douglas had lied to the audience in Ottawa. The resolutions Douglas had referred to had been written in a meeting Lincoln hadn't even known about until after the debate in Ottawa.

Lincoln said that his opponent had abandoned any notion of fair play.

> When the whole matter turns out as it does, and when we consider who Judge Douglas is—that he is a distinguished senator of the United States; that he has served nearly twelve years as such; that his character is not at all limited as an ordinary senator of the United States, but that his name has become of world-wide renown—it is most extraordinary that he should so far forget all suggestions of justice to an adversary.

Having been caught in a lie, Douglas tried to dodge the bullet. Knowing that a swift attack was better than a weak defense, he baited Lincoln, suggesting that he was a turncoat and a radical.

The audience, scorning Douglas's unwillingness to face fair criticism, taunted him. Douglas echoed his response to the groans and catcalls that had been hurled at him in 1854 in Chicago. He spoke sarcastically of black activist Frederick Douglass and then, warming to his subject, added, "All I have to say of it is this, that if you Black Republicans think that a negro ought to be on a social equality with your wives and daughters, and ride in a carriage with your wife, whilst you drive the team, you have a perfect right to do so." When his tormentors showed no mercy, he raised his chin and said defiantly, "I have seen your mobs before and I defy your wrath."

Lincoln pressed his advantage. Both men were clever lawyers, but in political campaigns, they talked to ordinary people—ordinary in the sense that they were people who applied themselves to problems that were practical: the raising of a barn, the mending of a harness or a plow, or the planting of a seed. Lincoln himself had been such a person, and he knew that he need not talk down to them.

In Freeport, Lincoln set a trap for Douglas. He asked a question Douglas had to answer, knowing that whichever way he answered, he was bound to hurt himself. The question, second in a list of four, sounded innocent enough. Could the voters of a territory exclude slavery "prior to the formation of a State Constitution"?

If Douglas said that voters could indeed so exclude slavery from a territory, Southerners would be enraged. Slaveholders wanted nothing more than to take their slaves anywhere they chose to take them. If they planned to spend a year or so in Massachusetts, New York, Illinois, or California, they might like to take half a dozen slaves with them, people who would groom their horses, clean their boots, and press their clothes. Hadn't the Dred Scott decision—declaring that black people had no rights—given them permission to do this?

The trouble was that Douglas, in defending the Kansas-Nebraska Act, had said repeatedly that voters in a territory had a right to decide things for themselves—a right to vote to make slavery legal *or* to exclude it. In order to be elected president of the United States in 1860, he would have to satisfy slaveholders and their friends; but in this case, in pleasing them, he would lose the respect of his constituents in central Illinois—people whose support he needed, first to be reelected to the Senate, then to be elected president. He was on the horns of a dilemma. If he answered yes to Lincoln's question, he would be cursed throughout the South. If he said no, he would be damned in Illinois.

Lincoln believed that Douglas, wanting to be president, would risk displeasing his constituents in Illinois and reach out to Southerners. He was wrong. Douglas said that, in his opinion, "the people of a Territory can, by lawful means, exclude slavery from their limits prior to the formation of a State Constitution."

Lincoln was of course surprised, and perhaps disappointed, but he

Lincoln at the time of his scheduled debates with Douglas, called "The Great Debates of 1858." This is one of only two or three full-length portraits of the sixteenth President. *The Library of Congress*

61

This poster, offering high prices for "No. 1" young men and women, is clear evidence that slavery was flourishing in 1853, in a state that never left the Union. *The collection of the author*

may have seen a glimmer of a hope that, in the end, he would profit from his own miscalculation.

For his performance in Freeport, Douglas was attacked by both abolitionists and Southerners. He was called "Little Trickster." It turned out that, in answering Lincoln's question as he had, he had lost his only chance of being elected president.

Jonesboro, in the narrow, southern part of Illinois, wedged between Missouri and Kentucky, had been settled mostly by people sympathetic to the South, people who had not owned slaves but disliked, and in some cases feared, black people. There, on September 15, Douglas, knowing Lincoln, temped him to foolishness by insisting that the founding fathers had *intended* to exclude black people from the Declaration of Independence.

Lincoln didn't take the bait. Facing such an audience, he knew it would be useless to declare his antislavery views. Picking up on the charge that he had been involved in a conspiracy to outlaw slavery everywhere, he restated his belief that, in states where slavery was entrenched, the federal government had no right to interfere with it.

Lincoln spent the night of September 17–18 in Mattoon. After breakfast, he and Douglas led a long procession east to Charleston. Farmers and townspeople made the twelve-mile journey with them, many on the backs of mules and horses, some high on the seats of carts and wagons. Others, grinding dust between their teeth, walked in the grass beside the road. As the leaders entered Charleston, they were joined by other pilgrims, some of whom had come across from Indiana.

★ 6 ★

SO SAD A FACE

Charleston was reportedly the first town in Illinois seen by the young Lincoln when he came across from Indiana. On September 18—the day of the fourth debate—an enormous banner hung across Main Street, bearing an illustration showing Lincoln driving several yoke of oxen. It read: OLD ABE THIRTY YEARS AGO. Racists had hung a competing banner picturing a white man, his black mate, and their child, captioned NEGRO EQUALITY, but Charleston's kinder citizens had torn it down.

After lunch, Lincoln and his opponent went to a clearing on the western edge of town, where a crowd greeted them with cheers and whistles. When the people settled down, Lincoln opened the discussion: "While I was at the hotel today, an elderly gentleman called upon me to know whether I was really in favor of producing a perfect equality between the negroes and white people. . . . I thought I would occupy perhaps five minutes in saying something in regard to it."

Lincoln said that, until he met the gentleman at the hotel, he hadn't planned to comment on the subject. One almost wishes he had not. In

Charleston, he revealed a prejudice that was common in his time and has, by no means, disappeared in ours. He said,

> I am not, nor have ever been, in favor of making voters or jurors of negroes, nor of qualifying them to hold office, nor to intermarry with white people; and I will say in addition to this that there is a physical difference between the white and black races which I believe will forever forbid the two races living together on terms of social and political equality.

Then he contradicted something he had said on July 10, in Chicago, where he had asked his countrymen to "discard all this quibbling about . . . this race and the other race and the other being inferior." In Charleston, he said, "And inasmuch as they cannot so live, while they remain together there must be the position of superior and inferior, and I as much as any other man am in favor of having the superior position assigned to the white race."

Most historians dismiss the notion that this blatant contradiction was based on political necessity. His detractors find it unforgivable. In any case, in his friendship with black leader Frederick Douglass, begun later in the White House, he revealed a change of heart.

In Charleston, Lincoln went on to discuss interracial marriage:

> I do not understand that because I do not want a negro woman for a slave I must necessarily want her for a wife. My understanding is that I can just let her alone. I am now in my fiftieth year, and I certainly never have had a black woman for either a slave or a wife. So it seems to me quite possible for us to get along without making either slaves or wives of negroes. . . . I have never had the least apprehension that I or my friends would marry negroes if there was no law to keep them from it; but as Judge Douglas and his friends seem to be in great apprehension that they might, if there was no law to keep them from it, I give him the

most solemn pledge that I will to the very last stand by the law of this State, which forbids the marrying of white people with negroes.

Six years later, when a friend asked Lincoln if he favored interracial marriage, his good-natured answer pointed to a change of attitude, if not a change of heart: "That's a democratic mode of producing good Union men, and I don't intend to infringe on the patent."

The fifth debate took place on October 7, in Galesburg—called by native son Carl Sandburg "a bright little prairie town." Galesburg, in Spoon River country, northwest of Peoria, hadn't just sprung up, as had many small towns in the West. It had been meticulously planned by its first settlers, most of them New Englanders. The coming of the railroad had later brought a rush of immigrants from Scandanavia, most of them opposed to slavery, as were early residents.

The debate was held on the campus of Knox College, where the two candidates drew an enormous and enthusiastic throng. As the two men took their places, a swift wind played with the flags and banners planted at the edges of the crowd.

At Knox College, Lincoln once again insisted on the inclusion of black people in Jefferson's immortal document and referred to the

Frederick Douglass in his early forties, probably in 1858. By 1858, when the Great Debates were in progress, he was prominent enough to be mentioned by Stephen Douglas. *The collection of the author*

Dred Scott decision made three years earlier. He said, "I believe the entire records of the world, from the date of the Declaration of Independence up to within three years ago, may be searched in vain for one single affirmation, from one single man, that the negro was not included in the Declaration of Independence."

The sixth debate was held in Quincy, on October 13. It was said of Quincy that it "begins at the Mississippi, hurdles steep bluffs, levels out on the uplands and trails off into woods and fields." Built on the site of what had been a village of Sauk Indians, it had become the largest city in the state and would remain so until after Lincoln's death. Its people manufactured wagons, carriages, farm machinery, and steam engines. Its farmers raised and exported tens of thousands of a breed of hog described as "long-legged, long-snouted and as fleet as deer."

In Quincy, Lincoln opened with familiar charges. At the end of his speech, he said that Douglas "had the high distinction, so far as I know, of never having said slavery is either right or wrong."

Unwilling to commit himself and further damage himself in the South, Douglas failed to deliver a direct reply, but he praised the Dred Scott decision as a thing from which there could be no appeal "this side of Heaven."

By the time the debates came to a close at Alton, where Elijah Lovejoy had been murdered, the candidates had long since made clear the substance of their arguments. Lincoln said, "The real issue of this controversy—the one pressing upon every mind—is the sentiment on the part of one class that looks upon the institution of slavery *as a wrong*, and of another class that *does not* look upon it as a wrong."

After the last debate, a friend talked to Lincoln in his hotel room. He long remembered Lincoln's look: "I never saw a more thoughtful face. I never saw a more dignified face. I never saw so sad a face."

Following the scheduled debates with Douglas, Lincoln spoke in other towns throughout the state. After speaking to a crowd in Petersburg, he and his friend Henry Villard, caught in a violent thunderstorm, took refuge in an empty boxcar. There, Lincoln told Villard that his highest political ambition was to be a senator from Illinois. He said that his wife insisted that he must be president. Then he added, "Just think of such a sucker as me as President!"

Though Lincoln failed to win a Senate seat, he remained a leader of his party and, as such, felt compelled to continue to express his views on what he saw as his nation's drift toward universal slavery. On a cold November day in 1859, he went west to Kansas Territory, to make speeches in town halls and auditoriums. En route to his first stop at Elwood, where he was scheduled to speak in the dining room of a hotel, he saw the cabins and sod houses of the poorest of the immigrants, thin wisps of smoke issuing from their crooked chimneys.

The territory had been, and still was, not just a haven for homesteaders, but a battleground for a bitter struggle over slavery. In 1854, the year the Kansas-Nebraska Act had been signed into law, the New England Emigrant Aid Company started sending antislavery people west to Kansas Territory so that when, at last, Kansas was admitted to the Union, it would be a free state. Other organizations—among them the New York Kansas League—did the same, but again, it was New Englanders who led the way. Most of these crusaders went to Lawrence, a town named for Amos Lawrence, treasurer of the New England organization.

The arrival of brave and vocal bands of antislavery folk frightened and enraged Missourians who supported slavery, and they, in turn, rallied around organizations with names like Sons of the South, Blue Lodge, and Social Band. Gangs of Missouri thugs, called "Border Ruffians," swarmed west, crossing into Kansas Territory, stuffing ballot boxes, burning barns and villages. They were so effective in intimidating and controlling voters that they engineered the passage of a law calling for the hanging of a person found with antislavery literature. A local reporter wrote, "The man who possesses a copy of *Uncle Tom's Cabin* is no better than a murderer."

It was in this atmosphere that, on May 23, 1856, a band of as many as a

Kansas Free State gunners. In 1856, when this photograph was taken, John Brown, captain of a Free State settlement at Osawatomie, slaughtered five proslavery settlers, people who themselves owned no slaves. *Kansas State Historical Society*

hundred Border Ruffians attacked the town of Lawrence. They brought with them two cannon and all manner of firearms, knives, and clubs. They terrorized and drove away the townspeople, leveled the Free State Hotel, and attacked the offices of the *Herald of Freedom*, smashing presses and scattering the newsprint and the type.

John Brown, who was captain of a free state settlement at Osawatomie, wasn't present at the sack of Lawrence, but he heard about it, and it made him angry. Proclaiming himself an instrument of God, he decided to attack a family of proslavery settlers. Before midnight on May 24, 1856, he and four of his sons and three comrades left Osawatomie in a wagon packed with food, camping gear, guns, and freshly sharpened swords. They traveled north, parked the wagon, took their weapons, and walked silently

John Brown as he looked when he was captain of a settlement at Osawatomie. Later, he grew a full beard. *National Archives*

to a cabin occupied by a man named Pleasant Doyle, his wife, and their three sons. These people were unarmed and owned no slaves. The youngest son, who was 16, reported later that their assailants "came into the house, handcuffed my father and two older brothers and started to take me, but my mother begged them to leave me as I would be all the protection she would have." Brown, his sons, and their accomplices took Doyle and his two older sons to a grassy knoll far enough from the house so their cries would not be heard and killed and butchered them. That same night, they moved along and butchered two more settlers.

Lincoln may or may not have known about Brown's murderous activities in Kansas Territory, but news of his raid on the United States Arsenal at Harpers Ferry—Brown's first move in starting what he hoped would be a successful war on slavery—was telegraphed to all sections of the country and reported in excruciating, if inaccurate, detail in newspapers coast to coast.

Several years before the raid, Brown had devised what he thought would be an effective strategy. At Harpers Ferry—on a point where the Shenandoah and Potomac Rivers meet—he would invade the U.S. arsenal and capture guns and ammunition, then go south, arming slaves as he went, setting off what he hoped would be a chain of slave uprisings.

He told Frederick Douglass what he planned to do, said that the Appalachian Mountains—which stretched from Maine to the Alabama border—might become an arrow that could penetrate the heart of slavery. He said that, at first, he could bring perhaps a hundred slaves to a hideout in the mountains.

These men, he believed, would go forth and bring in several thousand more, until he had at his command a vast liberating army.

Douglass believed that, even if Brown's raid succeeded, his small initial force would attract wide attention and would soon be hunted down and captured. Asked to join Brown's expedition, Douglass hesitated, then refused.

On the evening of October 16, 1859, a Sunday, Brown led twenty-one men—two of whom were sons of his and five of whom were black—against the arsenal. Taking its defenders by surprise, he and his men occupied a machine shop, a warehouse, and what was called an "engine house"—a building filled with firefighting apparatus—where the attackers kept their prisoners. That night, a small band of private citizens fired on the invaders.

At dawn on October 17, a church bell tolled, warning distant residents that something was amiss. When the news of the taking of the arsenal

Drawing of the fighting at the engine house at Harpers Ferry in 1859. *Leslie's Weekly*, 1859. *The collection of the author*

This painting of John Brown was based on a photograph taken in Boston, in the spring of 1859, five months before his raid on the arsenal at Harpers Ferry. *Williams College Sawyer Library*

reached the White House, President James Buchanan sent a force of U.S. Marines, commanded by Colonel Robert E. Lee, to the stronghold. Lee forced Brown to surrender. Brown lost sixteen men, killed outright. Others managed to escape. Some of these were recaptured. Four of Lee's men lost their lives, and one of Brown's sharpshooters killed an innocent onlooker. Brown was wounded. One of his captors asked him, "On what principle do you justify your acts?"

Brown answered, "Upon the Golden Rule. I pity the poor in bondage that have none to help them; that is why I am here; not to gratify any personal animosity, revenge or vindictive spirit. . . . You may dispose of me easily but this question is still to be settled—this Negro question—the end of that is still not yet."

It was said that Brown, sitting on his own rough casket while he waited to be hanged, stared at the hard blue sky and the ridges of the distant mountains and remarked, "This is, indeed, a beautiful country."

Brown was hanged in Charles Town, Virginia,* on December 2. Lincoln, still in Kansas Territory, mentioned him in Elwood and again in Leavenworth. In Elwood, he said, "John Brown has shown great courage, rare unselfishness. . . ." On December 3, in Leavenworth, Lincoln said, "Old John Brown has just been executed for treason against a state. We cannot object,

*Charles Town is now in West Virginia, which became a separate state in 1863.

even though he agreed with us in thinking slavery wrong. That cannot excuse violence, bloodshed, and treason."

Following his successful jousts with Stephen Douglas, in debate and repeatedly in less formal situations, Lincoln was the vice presidential choice of two presidential hopefuls: Salmon Chase and Simon Cameron. Lincoln, who had scoffed at the notion that he might be qualified to be elected president, was edging toward a change of mind.

★ 7 ★

RIGHT MAKES MIGHT

It was a sign of Lincoln's growing prominence that, in the fall of 1859, a committee of New Yorkers invited him to speak at Henry Ward Beecher's* Plymouth Church, in Brooklyn—now part of New York City, then the third-largest city in the country.

William Herndon reports that, after Lincoln received the invitation, he "came into the office and looked much pleased, not to say tickled. He said to me, 'Billy, I am invited or solicited to deliver a lecture in New York. Should I go?'"

"By all means," Herndon answered.

"If you were in my fix, what subject would you choose?"

Herndon said that the address should be political. "That's your forte."

Lincoln had three months to think about, write, and revise the speech. He went to work in the Illinois State Historical Library, reviewing founding documents and pondering the amendments to the Constitution that comprise the Bill of Rights. He gave close attention to transcripts of arguments made at the

*Beecher was a preacher, abolitionist, and champion of women's rights.

74

Constitutional Convention and debates and resolutions made in state
conventions on the composition of
the Constitution.

In the days before he left Springfield, Lincoln bought himself a new
black suit and new white shirts. His
friend Fleurville trimmed his hair.

On Thursday, February 23, he
began the journey east. In one railcar
then another, he worked on his speech
and slept. By Saturday, when his train
pulled into the New Jersey Railroad
Depot, the men on the committee had
changed the site of his address from
Plymouth Church to the Great Hall of
Cooper Union—a free public college
opened several months before.

An engraving from a photograph probably
taken in Peoria, Illinois, on May 20, 1860,
three months after Lincoln spoke at
Cooper Union. *Williams College Sawyer
Library*

Committee members met Lincoln
at a Hudson River ferry slip, told him about the change in plan, and took him
to the Astor House, a plush hotel at 221 Broadway. There, Lincoln was un-
daunted by the dark oak paneling and polished brass and the menu—part of
which was in French and included oysters, several kinds of duck, and an assortment of desserts. Sometimes he spoke more like a farmer than a potential
presidential candidate. At noon, in the dining room, an admirer came to
shake his hand, and Lincoln introduced a friend of his as a Democrat but "a
man so good tempered that he and I could eat out of the same rack, without
a pole between us."

That afternoon, he went to the newsroom of the *New York Independent*,
where he talked to editor Henry C. Bowen. On Sunday, he worked again on
his speech, refining it for the city's most distinguished businessmen, educa-

tors, publishers, and politicians and their visitors from other states. On Monday, he received at least twenty callers.

Monday evening, after supper, as his carriage made its way along Broadway and Astor Place to Cooper Square, snowflakes blew down from the rooftops, sifted over horsecars, carriages, and wagons. The air was cold, but a gathering of people waited in the yellow light of lanterns at the entrance to the massive brownstone building, hoping they might catch a glimpse of prominent New Yorkers and two famous antislavery leaders: Congressman Francis P. Blair Jr., of Missouri, and Kentuckian Cassius M. Clay, publisher of the *True American.* But, above all, the people hoped they might have a look at Lincoln. They were not disappointed. As he stepped down from his carriage, he was more than a head taller than most people in the crowd.

Lincoln was introduced by William Cullen Bryant, the proprietor and editor of the New York *Evening Post.* Bryant was also a noted man of letters. He wrote reviews, poetry and recollections. *National Archives*

Inside the hall, George P. Putnam Jr., son of a book publisher, was unimpressed by the appearance of the man from Illinois. He wrote about Lincoln's long, awkward figure, said that his clothes, "new for the trip, were evidently the work of an unskilled tailor." Putnam remembered "the large feet, the clumsy hands, the . . . gaunt head capped by a shock of hair that seemed not to have been thoroughly brushed out." He and other members of the audience expected an address as rustic as the man himself.

Lincoln was escorted to the platform by lawyer David Dudley Field and Horace Greeley, founder and editor of the New York *Tribune.* Other men spoke before him. At last, he was introduced by

William Cullen Bryant, proprietor and editor of the New York *Evening Post*.

As usual, Lincoln started on a high note, but he soon found his voice and began to win his audience. He presented a familiar recitation of his differences with Stephen Douglas over slavery. Then, in a direct appeal to the people of the South, he pointed out that George Washington had approved and signed an act of Congress outlawing slavery in the vast Northwest Territory—at that time the only territory owned by the United States. This, Lincoln said, was a precedent that should be honored and extended.

Still speaking to the people of the South, he said that they thought they were "conservative—eminently conservative—while we are revolutionary, destructive, or something of the sort." He

Horace Greeley was one of several men who escorted Lincoln to the platform in the Great Hall. In 1841, he founded the New York *Tribune* and, during the Civil War, prompted Lincoln to reply to his sometimes bitter editorials. *National Archives*

went on to say that it was he who was conservative because he followed the intentions of the founding fathers.

Probably unaware that he was skating on thin ice, Lincoln set out to defend his party.

> You charge that we stir up insurrections among your slaves. We deny it; and what is your proof? Harpers Ferry! John Brown!! John Brown was no Republican; and you have failed to implicate a single Republican in his Harpers Ferry enterprise. If any member of our party is guilty in that matter, you know it, or you do not know it. If you do know it, you are inexcusable for not designating the man and proving the fact. If you do

not know it, you are inexcusable for asserting it, and especially for persisting in the assertion after you have tried and failed to make the proof. You need not be told that persisting in a charge which one does not know to be true, is simply malicious slander.

Page one of a printed copy of what is now known as Lincoln's Cooper Union Address. Published by the Republican Executive Congressional Committee, this became an 1860 campaign document. Lincoln believed that, in his speech, he had vindicated all Republicans of the charge that they had supported John Brown's raid on Harpers Ferry when, in fact, many members of his party had supported Brown. *The Williams College Chapin Library*

In fact, there were Republicans, and many men and women who became Republicans, who gave John Brown both encouragement and money. Businessman John Murray Forbes and lawyer John Albion Andrew—an avowed Republican who in 1861 became governor of Massachusetts—supported Brown openly. Others who supported Brown were philanthropist Gerrit Smith, journalist Franklin Sandborn, businessman George L. Stearns, preacher and activist Thomas Wentworth Higginson, physician Samuel G. Howe, and Theodore Parker. These men were later called the "Secret Six." John Brown himself had toured New England and New York, raising money from a wide variety of antislavery people, many of whom were no doubt Republicans. While Andrew didn't fund Brown's raid on the arsenal at Harpers Ferry, he did give him encouragement and, after Brown was imprisoned, appealed to Republican Montgomery Blair to organize Brown's defense. He contributed to that defense, and after Brown was convicted and was sentenced to be hanged, called a meeting to raise money for Brown's wife and children. The meeting—held in Boston's Tremont Temple—featured speeches by a host of prominent reformers, among them poet and essayist Ralph Waldo Emerson, novelist Lydia Maria Child, and members of the Secret Six. All praised Brown. Andrew said that Brown's methods might be questioned, but that "John Brown himself is right. I sympathize with the man. I sympathize with his idea." Emerson, going a step further, said that Brown had "made the gallows as glorious as the cross."

At Cooper Union, Lincoln said,

> Slave insurrections are no more common now than they were before the Republican party was organized. What induced the Southampton insurrection, twenty-eight years ago, in which at least three times as many lives were lost as at Harpers Ferry? You can scarcely stretch your very elastic fancy to the conclusion that Southampton was "got up by Black Republicans."

Nat Turner's slave uprising, in Southampton County in Virginia in 1831, was, without question, the bloodiest slave revolt in the history of the nation. The insurrection was remarkable because it took place in a rural region marked by orchards and cotton and tobacco fields, a region where slave owners saw no reason to believe that their slaves were anything but happy.

Turner was a preacher, given to hallucinations. Like John Brown, who was to follow him, he imagined that he took his orders straight from God. He and six other slaves—all owned by the same master—hatched their conspiracy in a woods on the shores of a swamp named Cabin Pond. A solar eclipse—together with a mist that swept across the countryside—produced an atmosphere that spoke to Turner, and on August 22, in the early morning hours, he and his accomplices began their raid.

An engraving of an illustration of Nat Turner in 1831, plotting the slave insurrection in Southampton County, Virginia, in which a large number of Virginians lost their lives. He was later captured, tried, and hanged. *The collection of the author*

First, they killed their owner, Joseph Travis, and his wife. Then, after they were joined by several dozen other slaves, they killed thirteen men, eighteen women, and twenty-four children. Soldiers hunted down and captured most of Turner's men but not before terrified white men had killed almost one hundred slaves, most of whom were innocent.

Lincoln argued that Nat Turner's insurrection had been sparked by a natural lust for freedom. Often as they might deny this, planters and their wives and overseers recognized and feared this natural inclination. Lincoln said,

> Much is said by Southern people about the affection of slaves for their masters and mistresses and part of it, at least, is true. A plot for an uprising could scarcely be devised and communicated to twenty individuals before some one of them, to save the life of a favorite master or mistress,

would divulge it. This is the rule and the slave revolution in Haiti was not an exception to it, but a case occurring under peculiar circumstances.

The leader of the Haitian revolution Lincoln was referring to was Toussaint L'Ouverture, a princely looking man who became a towering hero, especially to black abolitionists. Toussaint L'Ouverture served his people as a surgeon, military strategist, and commander. In 1791, he took part in a revolution against both slavery and French rule. His army triumphed in the field, and he became the leader of a people's government. In 1802, Napoleon Bonaparte, in an effort to reestablish slavery on the island, captured him, charged him with conspiracy, and imprisoned him in France, where he died.

Lincoln warned that slave uprisings and attempts to foment them were unlikely to abolish slavery. "Whoever much fears, or much hopes, for such an event, will be alike disappointed."

Lincoln expressed, as he had many times, the hope that a peaceful resolution would appear. Again, he quoted Thomas Jefferson: "It is still in our power to direct the process of emancipation and deportation peacefully, and in such slow degrees, as that the evil will wear off insensibly. . . . If, on the contrary, it is left to force itself on, human nature must shudder at the prospect held up."

Again, speaking to the people of the South, Lincoln said, "Your purpose, then, plainly stated, is that you will destroy the government, unless you be allowed to construe and force the Constitution as you please, on all points in dispute between you and us. You will rule or ruin. . . ."

He pointed out what everyone in the Great Hall and most people in the country as a whole knew to be true: that the South would not abide the election of a Republican president. To the people of the South, he said, "In that supposed event, you say, you will destroy the Union; and then, you say, the great crime of having destroyed it will be upon us! That is cool. A highwayman holds a pistol to my ear, and mutters through his teeth, 'Stand and deliver, or I shall kill you, and then you will be a murderer!'"

His final words were, "Let us have faith that right makes might, and in that faith let us to the end dare to do our duty as we understand it."

Lincoln's friend Mason Brayman, who was with him in New York, said that Lincoln "held the vast meeting spellbound." This seems to have been the case. Certainly, Lincoln's speech at Cooper Union played an important, if not a vital, role in his success at the National Republican Convention held in what was called the "Great Wigwam" in Chicago.

Lincoln went from New York to New England, where he gave a series of effective speeches and took time to visit his son Robert, who was then a student at Phillips Exeter Academy in New Hampshire.

Published in *Harper's Weekly* in 1860, this cartoon illustrates the horrors of disunion, as the eagle and the serpent enter combat and symbols of democracy and liberty lie on the ground. *Williams College Sawyer Library*

Lincoln wasn't present in Chicago in the fall of 1860, when he was nominated by his party as its candidate for president, nor did he go to Chicago after he was nominated.

Chicago put on a lavish show for what one observer called the "very flower of the leaders of the Young Republican party." Delegates came to the city not just from Western and Northeastern states, but from Kentucky, Maryland, Virginia, Missouri, and Texas.

The Great Wigwam was a huge, hastily constructed building on Lake

Street. A reporter for the *Press and Tribune* wrote that it was lit at night "from turret to foundation . . . by a thousand lights." Over the main door was an immense translucent sign that read FOR PRESIDENT, HONEST OLD ABE. FOR VICE PRESIDENT, HANNIBAL HAMLIN.*

Proprietors of Chicago's boardinghouses and hotels turned away at least a thousand visitors. Some delegates spent their nights on billiard tables; others slept on pleasure boats, docked on the waterfront. Street parades, featuring military bands and floats, were so numerous that they sometimes bore down on one another. These near collisions brought on fistfights in the streets.

Because Douglas was unpopular in the South and had lost ground in his home state, his party was in trouble. Republicans had every reason to believe that they might win in the next presidential contest. They were anxious to put forward someone who could take advantage of their party's unexpected strength.

By May 15, it was clear that the contest was between two aspirants: William H. Seward and Abraham Lincoln. Of the two, Seward, who had been governor of New York State and twelve years a senator, was the more distinguished man. Moreover, like Lincoln, he had been a consistent enemy of slavery. In fact, he believed that slave states and free states were locked in what he called an "irrepressible conflict."

Lincoln, who had kept his distance so he wouldn't have to face people who would ask him to trade promises for votes, would have been furious had he known that several of the men who represented him at the convention, afraid that Seward's people would outnumber theirs, printed blocks of bogus tickets and gave them to Lincoln supporters who went early to the hall and took seats that would otherwise have been occupied by Seward delegates.

No doubt, Lincoln's managers made promises they couldn't keep, and Seward's men may well have done the same. In any case, on the third ballot, Lincoln took the lead and held it.

---

*Hamlin had been an antislavery congressman and senator and a governor of Maine. He served as vice president until 1865.

Lincoln's victory sparked a widespread celebration. A reporter for the *Press and Tribune* wrote about the tumult in the streets: "Cannon boomed. Men took up the cry for 'Old Abe' and it echoed and re-echoed throughout the city, the news flashed by telegraph to a waiting country."

One of Lincoln's managers, who may or may not have played a part in printing and distributing bogus tickets, made a statement about agreements made in what were later called "smoke-filled rooms." He said, "Mr. Lincoln is committed to no one on earth. . . . He has promised nothing." Lincoln, who had stayed in Springfield throughout the Wigwam circus, believed that he was free of dishonorable commitments.

A delegation went to Springfield to give Lincoln formal notice of his triumph in Chicago. Toward the end of their visit, Lincoln turned to William D. Kelley—a lanky member of the group—and asked him how tall he was.

William Henry Seward at the age of forty, when he was governor of New York State. Later, he was an antislavery senator. He opposed Lincoln in the 1860 presidential contest, then served in Lincoln's cabinet. Engraving from a portrait by Henry Inman. *Williams College Sawyer Library*

"Six feet three," came the answer.

Smiling, Lincoln said, "I beat you. I'm six feet four, without my high-heeled boots."

With a good-natured nod, Kelley said, "I am glad that we have found a candidate for the Presidency whom we can look up to."

There were many prominent black people who could find no reason to look up to Lincoln. To begin with, in the South, no black man—free or slave—so much as dared to hope that he would ever have the vote. No woman—black or white—had the vote. Connecticut denied black men the right to vote. Other New England states—Maine, Vermont, New Hampshire, Massachusetts, and Rhode Island—led the country in awarding their black citizens the privilege of marking ballots on election days. If they owned sufficient property, black men could vote in New York State. In Ohio, voters must appear to be more white than black. It was almost better not to vote than to have one's racial mixture judged by a narrow-minded bureaucrat.

Free black leaders voiced their disappointment over what to them was a poor choice. They would have preferred a radical or a moderate but less compliant candidate like Seward. If it was rumored that

Lincoln's letter of acceptance of the nomination of the Republican National Convention. The letter to George Ashmun, President of the Convention, is dated May 23, 1860. *Williams College Sawyer Library*

Republicans, if elected, would abolish slavery and extend equal rights to all black people, Republicans themselves were quick to deny the rumor. Thirty-five-year-old black Massachusetts doctor, teacher, and lawyer John Rock, while admitting that Republicans were opposed to the spread of slavery, said that few were in truth abolitionists:

> They go against slavery only so far as slavery goes against their interests; and if they keep on lowering their standards, as they have been for the last few months, they will soon say in New England, what they have already said in the Middle States, that the Republican Party is not only the

85

white man's party, but that it aims to place white men and white labor *against* black men and black labor.

Illinois black leader H. Ford Douglass said,

> Take Abraham Lincoln. I want to know if any man can tell me the dif-
> ference between the anti-slavery of Abraham Lincoln, and the anti-
> slavery of the old Whig party, or the anti-slavery of Henry Clay? Why,
> there is no difference between them. Abraham Lincoln is simply a
> Henry Clay Whig, and he believes just as Henry Clay believed in regard
> to this question. And Henry Clay was just as odious to the anti-slavery
> cause and anti-slavery men as ever was John C. Calhoun.

Referring to civil rights outrages, including the denial of the right to vote, he added, "I care nothing about that anti-slavery which wants to make the Territories free, while it is unwilling to extend to me, as a man, in the free States, all the rights of a man."

Publisher, journalist, and civil rights lecturer Frederick Douglass—the most prominent black leader of his century—who at first supported Lincoln, said as the campaign progressed, "Even the sentiments of the Republican party, as expressed by its leaders, have become visibly *thin* and *insipid.* . . . It promises to be about as good a Southern party as either wing of the old Democratic party." Deciding not to vote for Lincoln, Douglass had words of praise for radical and independent Gerrit Smith, who had no chance of appearing on the ballot. "Ten thousand votes for Gerrit Smith would do more, in our judgement, for the ultimate abolition of slavery in this country, than two million for Abraham Lincoln."

Other black Americans gave the Republicans a chance to prove themselves. Samuel Smothers, who taught school in Indiana, said, "The best antislavery

OPPOSITE: Campaign banner by Currier and Ives. Hamlin had been an antislavery congressman and senator and a governor of Maine. *National Portrait Gallery, Smithsonian Institution*

men in the nation are rallying under the Republican banner. This causes us to look hopefully to the Republican party for the ultimate abolition of slavery throughout the entire nation, and the elevation of our race to social and political equality."

After Lincoln won the presidency,* Frederick Douglass changed his mind. In doing so, he demonstrated his developed wisdom and his penetrating foresight. He wrote,

> What then has been gained to the anti-slavery cause by the election of Mr. Lincoln? Not much, in itself considered, but very much when viewed in the light of its relations and bearings. For fifty years the country has taken the law from the lips of an exacting, haughty and imperious slave oligarchy. The masters of slaves have been the masters of the Republic. Their authority was almost undisputed, and their power irresistible. They were the President makers of the Republic, and no aspirant dared to hope for success against their frown. Lincoln's election has vitiated their authority and broken their power. It has taught the North its strength, and shown the South its weakness. More important still, it has demonstrated the possibility of electing, if not an Abolitionist, at least an *anti-slavery reputation* to the Presidency.

---

*Lincoln gained only a plurality in a four-way race in which he was pitted against his perennial opponent Democrat Stephen Douglas, Southern faction Democrat John C. Breckinridge, and Constitutional Union Party candidate John Bell, who—like Breckinridge—took a Southern view of slavery.

⋆ **8** ⋆

THE MYSTIC CHORDS OF MEMORY

Lincoln said good-bye to Herndon on a Sunday afternoon, more than three months after the election. The partners met in their office, where they talked about their years together and the future of their practice. Lincoln was relaxed and in a cheerful frame of mind. Years later, Herndon wrote that, when they had finished talking business, Lincoln stretched out on the sofa. He asked, "Billy, how long have we been together?"

"Over sixteen years."

"We've never had a cross word during all that time, have we?"

"No, indeed we have not."

They talked a little longer, then, as Lincoln left the office, he asked Herndon to keep both their names on a sign that was swinging by its rusty hinges, at the foot of the stairway. "Give our clients to understand that the election of a President makes no change in the firm of Lincoln and Herndon. If I live, I'm coming back some time, and then we'll go right on practicing law as if nothing had happened."

With Lincoln Monday morning, in the chilly railroad station waiting for his train to come, were Mary; their three sons, Robert, Willie, and Tad;

Lincoln, in a white suit, standing by the doorway of his house in Springfield. Following his nomination, friends and neighbors paused to pay homage to the candidate. On the second floor, in the second window from the left, Willie Lincoln looks down at the crowd. In the decorated wagon in the foreground sit thirty-three young women, each representing one of the existing states. By an unknown photographer. *Courtesy of the Illinois State Historical Library*

and an entourage that included friends, bodyguards, and his two secretaries, John G. Nicolay and John Hay, both of whom were still in their twenties.

The train arrived, the screech of its brakes and the pealing of its bell drowning out all conversation. Outside, a light drizzle settled on the hats and shoulders of the people who had come to say good-bye. Lincoln and his party climbed aboard, and he went back to the observation platform so that he could say a few words to his friends and neighbors. One of them remembered that his "breast heaved with emotion and he could scarcely command his feelings sufficiently to commence."

At last in control of his breathing, he expressed great sadness at the parting.

> To this place, and the kindness of these people, I owe every thing. Here I have lived a quarter of a century, and have passed from a young to an old man. Here my children have been born, and one is buried. I now leave, not knowing when, or whether ever, I may return, with a task before me greater than that which rested upon Washington. Without the assistance of that Divine Being, who ever attended him, I cannot succeed. With that assistance I cannot fail. Trusting in Him, who can go with me, and remain with you and be everywhere for good, let us confidently hope that all will yet be well. To His care commending you, as I hope your prayers will commend me, I bid you an affectionate farewell.

During the long journey to his nation's capital, Lincoln stopped many times to give speeches, few of which were memorable. In most places, he told jokes and exchanged pleasantries, but at Independence Hall, in Phildelphia, he expressed his devotion to his country, to the Union. He said that his loyalty stemmed directly from the sentiments expressed in the Declaration of Independence. "I have pondered over the toils that were endured by the officers and soldiers of the army who achieved that independence. . . ." He praised the dedication of those patriots to the principles embodied in the Declaration. He said that he would sooner die than give up those principles.

Because his military aides told him that a plot against his life was afoot in Baltimore, he left the presidential train and entered Washington at night. He was met by his friend Elihu Washburne, who went with him to Willard's Hotel where, insofar as possible, he behaved like any other guest. Illustrator and cartoonist Thomas Nast drew a picture of him sitting in the lobby of the Willard, calmly reading a newspaper. Aware of his undignified arrival, others pictured him sneaking into Washington in ridiculous disguises.

The unfinished capitol. *National Archives*

On his first day in Washington, Lincoln drove with Seward to the White House, where he talked to President Buchanan. He revisited the Capitol. The dome that was to crown the building was unfinished. In its place was a steel structure, dark against the winter sky. In the legislative chambers, he was greeted warmly by old friends and was scorned by a few ungracious Democratic senators and congressmen, some of whom refused to speak to him.

As Lincoln faced ten days of waiting to be inaugurated as the sixteenth president of the United States, the federal government was tottering. Two months before, South Carolina had cut ties to the Union, an example followed by Mississippi, Florida, Alabama, Georgia, Louisiana, and Texas. Delegates from six of these seven states had met in Alabama* and had formed a rebel government, a government pledged to honor and respect slaveholders and promote the spread of slavery. They called themselves the "Confederate States of

*Texas was the last of these states to secede and sent no delegate.

America"—or the Confederacy. Jefferson Davis, who had graduated from West Point and had been a soldier, senator, and secretary of war, had been sworn in as its president. Lincoln had been saddened by the news that Davis's vice president was the tiny, almost skeletal Alexander Stephens, a man he knew and liked and had hoped would be loyal to the federal government. The Confederacy, never recognized by Lincoln, marched under its own flag—the stars and bars. As Lincoln was soon to say, "A disruption of the Federal Union, heretofore only menaced, is now formidably attempted."

During the four months in which Lincoln had waited to take office, things had gone from bad to worse. President Buchanan's secretary of war was a loyal Southerner and had allowed arms and ammunition to be shipped south to the states in rebellion. Federal strongholds—U.S. coastal forts, arsenals, and barracks—had been engulfed by the Confederacy at the same time that the federal

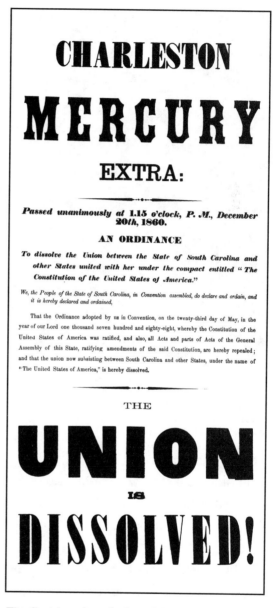

The first imprint of a broadside advertising an extra edition of the *Charleston Mercury*, proclaiming dissolution of the Union. South Carolina left the Union more than two months before Lincoln was inaugurated. Other states followed suit. *Williams College Chapin Library*

Jefferson Davis, President of the Confederate States of America. Lincoln never recognized the Confederate government. He sometimes referred to it as the "Rebel government." *National Archives*

government, while in Buchanan's hands, had done little to prepare itself for civil war.

Batteries at Charleston, South Carolina, had fired on the merchant ship, *Star of the West*, come to reinforce Fort Sumter, which stood on a shoal in the mouth of Charleston Harbor. The big guns around the harbor had forced the ship to sail away, and Buchanan had decided to do nothing to retaliate. The *Rhoda B. Shannon,* a trim little schooner bound from Boston to Savannah, would soon venture into Charleston Harbor and, like the larger ship, would be fired on and would retreat.

The fort was occupied and defended by Unionist Major Robert Anderson, but Anderson, under siege since December, was short of food and ammunition; if relief was not forthcoming soon, he would be forced to surrender.

Under these circumstances, Lincoln would have little time to think of slavery as a moral issue. It was all very well for abolitionists to demand that slavery be outlawed, but it was clear to Lincoln that any statement he might make would be useless if not backed by overwhelming military force. In the spring of 1861, the federal government was not prepared to dictate to the South.

Some abolitionists—among them William Lloyd Garrison—had favored a division of the Union. They had reasoned that the South was engaged in evil practices and so should be severed from the Union, as a surgeon might cut off a wounded arm or an infected leg. Not only did Lincoln see that this would strand four million slaves and their unborn children and grandchildren, but he believed that North and South were interlocking segments of a single nation. He was convinced that no confederacy of states, north or south, had the right to break the ties gathered and secured by the founders of American democracy. He was determined to use every means at his command to make his nation whole again. As he made this decision, he realized that civil war would be much more complicated than a war with a single hostile foreign power. In 1861, the Union looked much like a house of cards; so as not to bring it down, he would have to compromise, not just once, but many times.

As war approached, Lincoln knew that, first of all, he must secure the loyalty of the people of the states not yet part of the Confederacy. So far, only states that comprised the Lower South had left the Union. Hanging in the balance were eight slave states: Missouri, Arkansas, Kentucky, Tennessee, North Carolina, Maryland, Delaware, and Virginia. It didn't take a military strategist to see that Maryland and Virginia, joining forces, could cut off and occupy Washington—a city guarded by no more than a scattering of federal troops. In any case, if all eight states left the Union, the North would probably lose the war, in which case democracy would lie in ruins, as would any effort to abolish slavery.

As he waited to take office, Lincoln filled his cabinet posts. He appointed seven men to advise him and to manage the departments of the government. Among these were Seward, secretary of state, and Simon Cameron, secretary of war, soon to be replaced by Edwin M. Stanton. In the ten days during which Lincoln stayed at the Willard, he and Mary welcomed streams of visitors and attended dozens of receptions. Most people meeting him for the first time were favorably impressed by him, but a prominent Virginian called him a cross between an Andalusian crane and a jackass, and thought that he was hypocritical and childish, "without manners, without moral grace."

British minister to Washington Richard B. Pemell, Lord Lyons, found him charming. Those candidates who had been defeated by him came to offer him encouragement. Stephen Douglas came to a reception for the Lincolns and renewed his pledge of loyalty to both Lincoln and the Union. To the president-elect, he said, "I am with you, Mr. President, and God bless you."

As Lincoln watched Douglas leave, he remarked, "What a noble man he is!"

Douglas was, indeed, eager to assist the man who had long been his rival. This he demonstrated in his speeches and in several meetings with the president-elect, whom he had begun to understand and to admire. He was soon to die of typhoid fever—at the age of forty-eight—with his devoted wife, Adele, at his bedside. There were those who thought that, had he lived, he might have stopped the rush toward war, but the time for his brand of compromise had long since passed.

On the morning of March 4, 1861, rain clouds moved slowly east, crossed the Potomac and the Chesapeake, and drifted out to sea. Intermittent sunlight was reflected in the buttons and the buckles of sharpshooters posted on the rooftops to protect the president and the president-elect. An open carriage flanked by several companies of infantry and cavalry carried Lincoln and Buchanan past the crowds lining Pennsylvania Avenue. Along the route, people cheered until they reached the Capitol. There, they entered a protected passageway leading to a temporary wooden platform, where Lincoln was to speak to his troubled fellow citizens.

After witnessing the swearing in of his vice president, Lincoln listened to a gracious introduction, then stood up. It was said that he fumbled with his hat and cane and that Stephen Douglas, who was sitting close to him, held them for him while he spoke. Lincoln set his reading glasses on the bridge of his nose, stood straight, and began to speak.

Remembering the need to make peace with the border states, he repeated a familiar promise: "I have no purpose, directly or indirectly, to interfere with the institution of slavery in the States where it exists. I believe I have no lawful right to do so. . . ."

He reaffirmed his willingness to enforce laws governing the return of fugitives. He said that the Constitution should be honored, until such time as unfair amendments be repealed. He said that the protection of the rights of states was necessary "to that balance of power on which the perfection and endurance of our political fabric depend."

Then he talked about the subject closest to his heart: law relating to the preservation of the Union.

> The Union is much older than the Constitution. It was formed, in fact, by the Articles of Association in 1774. It was matured and continued by the Declaration of Independence in 1776. It was further matured, and the faith of all the then thirteen States expressly plighted and engaged that it should be perpetual, in the Articles of Confederation in 1778.

He said that the drafting of the Constitution, in 1787, had created a more perfect Union. He argued that there was no law—or loophole in any law—that permitted the destruction of the federal government. He declared that, in spite of the rebellion of the Southern states, the Union still existed and was obligated to defend and to maintain itself. He said that "there needs be no bloodshed or violence; and there shall be none, unless it be forced on the national authority."

In view of the precarious position of the Southern strongholds, especially that of Fort Sumter, he said, "The power confided in me will be used to hold, occupy, and possess the property and places belonging to the government. . . ."

As he had done at Cooper Union, he appealed directly to the people of the South. "Before entering upon so grave a matter as the destruction of our national fabric, with all its benefits, its memories, and its hopes, would it not be wise to ascertain precisely why we do it?" He struck a note of desperate pleading. "Will you, while the certain ills you fly to are greater than all the real ones you fly from—will you risk the commission of so fearful a mistake?"

He called secession nothing short of anarchy. Then he returned to a familiar observation: "One section of our country believes slavery is right, and ought to be extended, while the other believes it is wrong, and ought not to be extended. This," he said, "is the only substantial dispute."

Whether slavery was right or wrong was indeed the overriding question, the question that had brought the nation to the verge of war. Lincoln had refused to compromise over its extension and, in time, would refuse to compromise over any part of it; but he followed Seward's wish that he extend an olive branch to the people of the South.

> I am loth to close. We are not enemies, but friends. We must not be enemies. Though passion may have strained, it must not break our bonds of affection. The mystic chords of memory, stretching from every battlefield and patriot grave to every living heart and hearthstone all over this broad land, will yet swell the chorus of the Union when again touched, as surely they will be, by the better angels of our nature.

Following the address, Lincoln was sworn in as his nation's sixteenth president.

The poetry and supplication of the final paragraph of his address were lost on an editor of the *Charleston Mercury*, who wrote that the words of "the Orang-Outang at the White House" were a vicious declaration. An observer in Ohio saw, as did many other journalists, that blood would soon stain the soil and darken all the waters of America. "Brother will be arrayed in hostile front against brother."

Black journalists found no reason to rejoice. The editors of the weekly *Anglo-African Magazine* expressed their disappointment in Lincoln's speech: "We gather no comfort from the inauguration of Abraham Lincoln."

No wonder. Half a loaf wouldn't satisfy a people whose government had long denied them any pretense of equality. In the eyes of black people, Lincoln rated little praise. Had he not said that he did not intend to interfere with slavery? Had he not stated his intention to uphold existing laws calling for the capture and return of fugitives? The *Anglo-African* pointed out that his repeated resolution to arrest the spread of slavery was inadequate at best. "It is the *existence* not the *extension* of slavery that is the issue."

Free black Americans continued to celebrate the deeds of men like Toussaint L'Ouverture, Nat Turner, Joseph Cinque,* and John Brown. Following years of argument and composition, they were ready to risk life and treasure to attain equality for themselves and to free their brothers in the South. The *Anglo-African* called for "the violent overthrow of slavery," and hoped for an uprising as swift as those "which had been the terror of European tyrants. . . . Only through the Red Sea of civil war and insurrection can the sins of this demonized people be washed away."

Mary Lincoln in the gown she wore at the time of the inaugural festivities. *National Archives*

While black abolitionists and journalists in the North expressed impatience, four million slaves in the South were listening and wondering. A mysterious network linked them to their brothers and their sisters in the North. Ignorant South Carolina slaves, some of them on isolated islands, heard that a man named Lincoln had been chosen president. Some said that he was black, but—black or white—he was a friend. Black people everywhere were already starting to love Lincoln. Some would soon discover that he was a mortal man, not an angel whose wings beat a song of freedom, but most believed that, in time, he would find a way to help them.

The morning after his inauguration, Lincoln read a report from Major Anderson, telling him that he needed not just food and ammunition, but an additional 20,000 men to hold Fort Sumter. Lincoln, having promised to defend

*In May 1839, in Cuban waters, African Joseph Cinque led a successful mutiny aboard the Spanish slave-ship *Amistad*. At the end of August, the ship was discovered lying at anchor off the east end of Long Island. Cinque and several dozen other mutineers were taken to nearby Connecticut and, in a long ensuing legal battle, were defended by a host of abolitionists. Eventually, the case was heard by the U.S. Supreme Court, where the closing arguments were delivered by John Quincy Adams. The mutineers were set free and Cinque returned to his home in Africa.

and, if possible, retake strongholds belonging to the federal government, knew that reinforcement of the fort would bring on war.

Lincoln was a lawyer and had been a legislator, but he had never had executive experience. As he faced a tidal wave of troubles, he took comfort from his talks with Secretary of State Seward, who, as Governor of New York State, had gained experience that Lincoln lacked. But Seward was ambitious, and it soon became apparent that he hoped to be a sort of shadow president. Seward was in favor of surrendering Fort Sumter, but Lincoln, by no means in Seward's pocket, listened to a great many other people. Lincoln's friend Francis P. Blair Sr. stormed into Lincoln's office and warned him that surrender of the fort was surrender of the Union, "tantamount to treason."

Those who, like Seward, believed that the fort should be abandoned

The bombardment of Fort Sumter, as imagined by an illustrator. Published shortly after the bombardment, the illustration shows what appears to be a dead Confederate soldier. In fact, no lives were lost on either side during the bombardment of the fort. *Library of Congress*

thought that, with its surrender, the rebellion would collapse; but Michigan's senator, Zachariah Chandler, told Lincoln that the time had come to confront the arrogance of the secessionists. Without risking bloodshed over a clear moral issue, what would the federal government be worth?

Lincoln clung to the view that peace might still be negotiable, but he realized that surrender of the fort would bring a weakening of resolution on the part of the people of the North and would be an open invitation to both France and England to recognize the rebel government. He understood these things, but, knowing that a move to bolster Sumter might begin a long and costly war, he remained in an agony of indecision.

In response to crisis and uncertainty, Lincoln sufffered from depression. He slept very little. He himself, as well as his government, was in trouble. People said that he looked haggard. At last, under crushing pressures, he decided he would reinforce Fort Sumter and so notified Francis W. Pickens, governor of South Carolina.

There was some negotiation, but it brought no agreement. South Carolinians were already bent on war. Without consultation with the other states of the Confederacy, they took action. At 4:30 A.M., on April 12, a flash of light, followed by a dull explosion, sent a mortar shell arching high across the sky. The shell exploded just above the fort. Then came the flashes of a cannonade. The big guns around the harbor cracked and boomed, sending out their fearsome message. Charleston's graceful houses shook as if in expectation of the terrors and the tragedies of a kind of warfare humankind had never seen before. Anderson and his men, close to starving, held the fort another day, another night, then surrendered.

As it became increasingly apparent that Virginia was about to cast its lot with the Confederacy, Lincoln called for 75,000 volunteers to defend the capital. He said in part, "I appeal to all loyal citizens to favor, facilitate, and aid this effort to maintain the honor, the integrity, and existence of our National Union, and perpetuity of popular government; and to redress wrongs already long enough endured."

Following the start of war and Lincoln's call for volunteers, four more states joined the Confederacy: Virginia, Arkansas, Tennessee, and North Carolina.

While the people of the South had fashioned uniforms, polished swords, and cleaned firearms, the people of the North hadn't quite known what was happening, and Lincoln had done little to enlighten them. His decision to enlist troops to defend nation's capital and, if possible, take back federal property, evoked in them a rush of confidence and patriotic fervor.

White men enlisted in large numbers. All who were fit, and many who were much too young to go to war, were accepted eagerly. Black men in the North, sensing that, at last, slavery might be abolished, gathered in public parks, empty halls, and dusty lots, drilled, and—when they could find a musket—practiced marksmanship. In a meeting at a Baptist church in Boston, several hundred black men voted to depart without delay. In Providence, a company of black soldiers was prepared to join the First Rhode Island Regiment. In New York, the response to Lincoln's call was heroic. There, hundreds of black citizens offered to recruit, equip, and train three regiments to rush to the defense of Washington. Two thousand met in a Masonic hall in Philadelphia. In Pittsburgh, black men organized what they called the "Hannibal Guards"; and in Chicago, Cleveland, and Detroit, black men prepared to go to war. Thousands of intelligent, physically imposing black Americans were ready to lay down their lives for the Union, but, because they were black, all were told that their services would not be needed.

Remembering slave uprisings, Southerners were afraid to arm their slaves, but they knew that they could use them to support their armies—use them as laborers, orderlies, blacksmiths, grooms, and cooks. Black men had fought courageously in other wars and were serving in the U.S. Navy, but, even so, many people in the North thought that they would turn and run at the first sound of cannon fire. Most believed that widespread use of black soldiers would be an experiment at best. In any case, with an eye on uncommitted states, all of which harbored slavery, Lincoln was far from ready to enlist large numbers of black men in the service of his government. So the war began

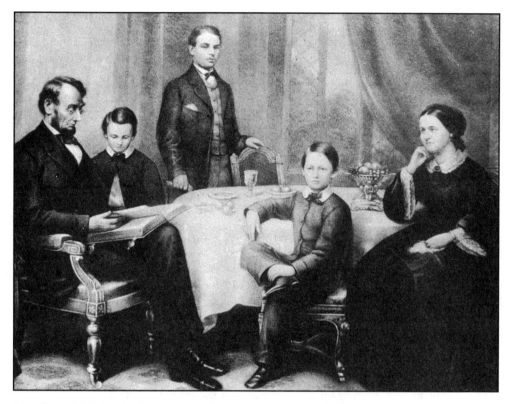

Lincoln and his family in the White House in 1861. Painting by Francis Bicknell, done from photographs and sketches. *Courtesy Lincoln Home National Historic Park*

without them. As late as the summer of 1862, when Indiana offered Lincoln two full regiments of black men, he said, "To arm the negroes would turn 50,000 bayonets from the loyal Border States against us that were for us."

The citizens of Maryland, still teetering between loyalty and treason, knew that they didn't like the sight of Yankee soldiers, black or white. When a white Massachusetts regiment marched through the streets of Baltimore—a secessionist stronghold—on the way to Washington, first blood was drawn when sharpshooters and street gangs wounded thirty-six federal soldiers and killed four of them outright.

In response to this attack on federal troops, Lincoln ordered the suspension of a basic right, a right guaranteed in England in 1674 and restated by the

framers of the Constitution. This right was defined in the writ of habeas cor-
pus, which provided that no person could be held in jail without a trial. In sus-
pending this right, Lincoln reasoned that anyone in rebellion against federal
laws could be forcibly detained. At first, the suspension of the writ applied
only to the people in a corridor between Washington and Philadelphia, a corridor through which federal troops must pass on their way to Washington.
More than a year later, Lincoln was to broaden the suspension to include all
states and territories and, in so doing, was to mandate the arrest of anyone
thought to be guilty of disloyalty to the Union.

New York's elite Seventh Regiment skirted Baltimore and arrived in Washington intact. On May 21, a private in the Seventh—later to command a regiment of black enlisted men—wrote that Lincoln had reviewed his regiment.
The president stood between his sons Tad and Willie, holding hands with both
of them. He was happy to see loyal soldiers coming to the capital:

> Old Abe stood out in front of us, looking as pleasant and kind as possi-
> ble, and when we presented arms, took off his hat in the most awkward
> way, putting it on again with his hand on the back of the rim, country
> fashion. A boy came up with a pail of water for us, and the President
> took a great swig from it as it passed. I couldn't help thinking of the im-
> mense responsiblity he has on his shoulders, as he stood there laughing
> and talking.

★ 9 ★

A TIME OF TIMES

At noon, on September 22, 1862, all seven of the president's close advisors joined him in his office, which served also as his cabinet room. They gathered at one end of a long, black walnut table, near his worn and cluttered desk.

All knew that this was not to be an ordinary meeting. So as to relieve the tension, Lincoln read aloud a story—"High-Handed Outrage at Utica" by humorist Artemis Ward—which he thought immensely funny. Stanton, who had by then replaced Cameron as secretary of war, sat unsmiling through the short recitation. Others, understanding Lincoln's need to relax and clear the air, laughed or nodded pleasantly.

Lincoln finished reading, then explained the purpose of the meeting. He said that he had been preoccupied with "the relation of the War to Slavery." He thought that the time had come to issue a proclamation dealing with that relation. He said, "I wish it were a better time."

In wishing it had been a better time, he was thinking of a battle fought five days before in Sharpsburg, Maryland. In the Battle of Antietam, a potentially overwhelming Union force under General George B. McClellan had compelled a Confederate army under General Robert E. Lee to withdraw and recross the Potomac. Lincoln knew that if McClellan had chased Lee, he could have captured him and his exhausted men and brought the Union to the verge of victory. But the most costly single day of fighting in the war had killed or wounded more than 23,000 soldiers—Union and Confederate—and produced little more than a standoff. A young Union officer long remembered what had followed the tumult: "At last night came on, and, with the exception of an occasional shot from the outposts, all was quiet. The crickets chirped, and the frogs croaked, just as if nothing had happened all day long, and presently the stars came out bright, and we lay down among the dead, and slept soundly until daylight."

As Lincoln talked to the members of his cabinet, he understated what he felt about McClellan's lack of fighting spirit. "The action of the army against the rebels has not been quite what I should have best liked. . . ."

Lincoln went on to say, "When the rebel army was at Frederick, I determined as soon as it should be driven out of Maryland to issue a proclamation of emancipation. . . ." Before he started reading what came to be called the "Preliminary Emancipation Proclamation," he added, "I do not wish your advice about the main matter—for that I have determined for myself."

It had taken Lincoln three months to complete the document he read aloud on September 22. In the spring of 1862, as he thought about its composition, he was in deep mourning for his third son, Willie, who had died on February 20, following an attack of typhoid fever. The death of Willie, who was bright and handsome, left the family devastated. When Lincoln looked down at his dead son's face, he said softly, "He was too good for this earth. . . ."

Later, Lincoln went to his office, and when the thin and bearded Nicolay rose to greet him, Lincoln said, "Well, Nicolay, my son is gone. . . ." Willie's funeral took place in a driving rain. In the time remaining to him, Lincoln sometimes shut himself away so that he could cry alone. As much as two years after Willie's death, continuing his practice of reciting passages from Shake-

On July 22, 1862, Lincoln read an early draft of his Emancipation Proclamation to the members of his cabinet. Exactly two months later, he read the Preliminary Emancipation Proclamation to a gathering of the same men. The final version of the proclamation was issued on January 1, 1863. This is a reproduction of a painting by Francis B. Carpenter, completed in 1864. In the painting, Edwin M. Stanton is seated on the left, his right arm resting on his chair. Salmon P. Chase stands beside him. William H. Seward sits in the foreground, facing Stanton, and behind him, left to right, are Gideon Welles, Caleb B. Smith, Montgomery Blair, and Edward Bates. *Library of Congress*

speare's plays, he was reading to a friend parts of *King John* and found himself face-to-face with the insistence of his grief.

> *And, father cardinal, I have heard you say*
> *That we shall know our friends in heaven:*
> *If that be true, I shall see my boy again.*

Such deep emotions were evoked by these lines that Lincoln bowed his head and sobbed uncontrollably.

It was Lincoln's habit to go every day to the War Department to read

Lincoln visiting McClellan following the Battle of Antietam. Lincoln knew that if McClellan had chased Lee, he could have destroyed Lee's army, but McClellan was content with what amounted to a standoff. *National Archives*

telegrams from his generals in the field and to send them orders and suggestions. Telegrapher Thomas Eckert, knowing that the president wanted to be left alone to work on an important paper, suggested that he use a desk in his office. It was at this desk that Lincoln wrote the Emancipation Proclamation.

On his first day at the desk, he wrote a line or two but spent a lot of time staring into space and thinking. For several minutes at a time, he studied the activities of a family of large spiders in a web above the desk.

As Lincoln wrote the Emancipation Proclamation, it was impossible for him to separate his feelings from his stated policies. He considered mostly military and political imperatives, but he must surely have been touched, at least to some extent, by his emotions. He had always hated slavery and his hatred had been deepened by the spectacle of slave markets in New Orleans, by the sight of men in chains on a steamboat bound from Louisville to St. Louis, and by his glimpses of the degradation of the people in slave pens in Washington. He must have been aware of the moral force of the paper he was working on.

As Lincoln worked, Eckert noticed that he read and repeatedly reread what he had written, carefully going over every sentence, often putting question marks in the margins. As he worked, precedent hung above him like the shadow of a man bending over a bright fire. Where slavery was concerned, his country had long lagged behind other nations. In Europe and in South America, governments that had once allowed the sale of captured Africans had done away with slavery. Russia was just taking final steps to free its serfs. In French and British colonies, including Canada, slavery had been eliminated by decree. Mexico had outlawed slavery. In the Western Hemisphere, it had lasted only in parts of the United States and in several of its territories and in both Brazil and Cuba.

As Lincoln faced his country's tardiness in eliminating slavery, he looked back on a year of military disappointments. In view of these disappointments, he knew how difficult it would be to retain the loyalty of the remaining border states—Missouri, Kentucky, Maryland, and Delaware—none of which had outlawed slavery. He knew that he must compromise in order to retain that loyalty so he decided he would let those states keep their slaves, at least until he had a chance to outlaw slavery everywhere.

During the three months Lincoln worked on the Emancipation Proclamation, he was constantly concerned about the progress of the war. At the beginning of the conflict, with several of his generals he had outlined a broad military strategy called the "Anaconda Plan," whose purpose was encirclement of the Confederacy. The plan called for a blockade of Southern ports on the Atlantic and Gulf Coasts and control of the Mississippi River. The blockade, Lincoln thought, would keep the ships of foreign powers—especially England, which maintained a naval base in Bermuda—from trading arms and ammunition for the products of the South. As it turned out, federal ships could only partially control the three thousand miles of coastal waters from the Chesapeake to the delta of the Mississippi river—one hundred miles or so southeast of New Orleans—and foreign and Confederate ships routinely penetrated the blockade.

Optimists had thought that federal troops could put down the rebellion in

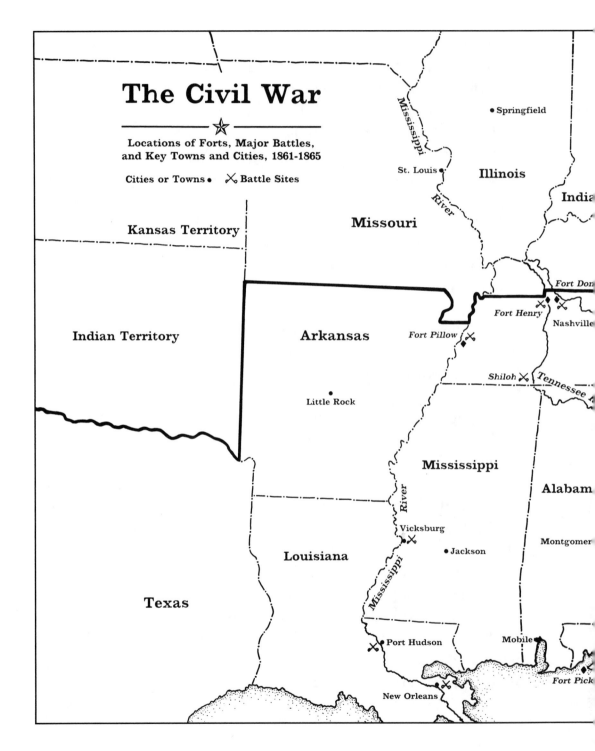

The Civil War

Locations of Forts, Major Battles,
and Key Towns and Cities, 1861-1865

Cities or Towns • ✕ Battle Sites

Kansas Territory

Missouri

• Springfield

Mississippi River

St. Louis •

Illinois

India

Indian Territory

Arkansas

Fort Don

Fort Henry

Nashville

Fort Pillow ✕

Shiloh ✕

Tennessee

• Little Rock

Mississippi

Alabam

Mississippi River

Vicksburg
• ✕

• Jackson

Montgomer

Louisiana

Texas

Mississippi

• Port Hudson ✕

Mobile •

Fort Pick

New Orleans ✕

LINCOLN AND SLAVERY

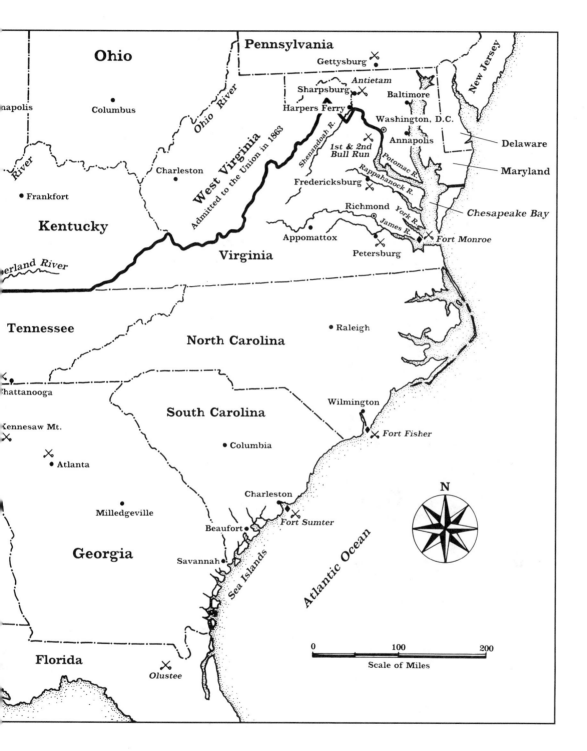

a month or two but, in the first major battle of the war—the first Battle of Bull Run—Union forces had been routed near a railroad junction in Virginia. In the West, things had gone a little better. In Tennessee, tough and aggressive General Ulysses S. Grant had captured two strategic river forts—Fort Henry and Fort Donelson—and, in a peach orchard close to Pittsburg Landing, Union soldiers, on the verge of defeat, had at last driven back Confederate soldiers in the cruel and costly Battle of Shiloh.

The trouble in the East had stemmed largely from McClellan's caution or, as Frederick Douglass had suggested, "traitorous inclinations." Because Lincoln had been urging him to attack the Confederate capital at Richmond, McClellan had organized and carried out an amphibious campaign that he reckoned would be safer than advancing over land. In what was known as the Peninsula or Peninsular campaign, he took 200,000 men down the Potomac to the Chesapeake, to a point between two rivers—the York and the James. His force was almost twice as large as that of his enemy, but he failed to move aggressively and, as was his custom, snatched defeat from the jaws of victory. Stopped by Robert E. Lee—by then in command of the Army of Northern Virginia—he put on a clean uniform, brushed his hair, and began an orderly retreat.

George B. McClellan, in his thirties when the Civil War was fought, was Lincoln's most exasperating general. Because he was afraid to fight, Frederick Douglass thought that he might have been a traitor. In any case, he thought himself superior to Lincoln and ran against him in the 1864 election. *National Archives*

Following a second rout of Union forces at Bull Run, Lee terrified the people of the North when he crossed the Potomac northwest of Washington in a move to destroy a main-line railroad bridge at Harrisburg—a vital link between the factories of the North and the Union armies in the West. If successful, he planned then to march on to Philadelphia, Baltimore, and Washington. There was talk that he might even be bold enough to move on to New York City. His plan, however, had been foiled at Sharpsburg, not by brave or clever generalship, but because his strategy had been revealed to McClellan* and because McClellan had a larger army whose supply lines were much shorter.

Since the beginning of the war, abolitionists both black and white had urged the president to free the slaves. First among black abolitionists was Frederick Douglass. Douglass, who had often criticized the president, urged immediate emancipation of all slaves and enlistment of black men in Union regiments. He wrote, "Jefferson Davis is a powerful man, but Jefferson Davis has no such power to blast the hope and

Charles Sumner in his fifties, when he knew the Lincoln family and talked often to the President, urging him to issue an emancipation proclamation. He never quite recovered from the wounds inflicted by Preston S. Brooks and died in his early sixties. *National Archives*

break down the strong heart of this nation, as that possessed and exercised by Abraham Lincoln." The people, Douglass said, had every right to hold the president "sternly responsible for any disaster or failure attending the suppression of this rebellion."

First among white abolitionists was Charles Sumner, back in action following a long recovery. Sumner had exerted gentle but relentless pressure on the President. In May 1861, he took an evening drive with Lincoln through the twilit streets of Washington. He told the president that he understood his cau-

---

*Lee's Special Order 191, containing his battle plans, was lost by a Confederate courier and found by a Union soldier, in a large envelope, wrapped around three cigars.

tion but suggested that he issue an emancipation proclamation. Lincoln told him that to issue such a proclamation following the first disastrous Battle of Bull Run would appear to be an act of desperation. He said he was determined to await a military victory.

A year or so before his death, Lincoln said of himself, "I claim not to have controlled events, but confess plainly that events have controlled me." The truth of this insight was never more apparent than it was during Lincoln's composition of the Emancipation Proclamation. Events not in any way precipitated by the president cleared the way for issuance of the Proclamation. The first of these was the passage by the Congress—on August 6, 1861—of the first Confiscation Act, which declared free all slaves whose owners had aided or were aiding the Confederacy.

At the same time, John Charles Frémont became the first of two of Lincoln's generals to issue an emancipation proclamation of his own. The high-spirited and independent Frémont was a popular explorer who had opened up the West and had helped secure what became the state of California. A politician as well as a soldier, he had been the first Republican candidate for president. On August 30—as commander of the Department of the West, and without consulting Lincoln—he declared that all slaves in every rebel state were free. Lincoln was on solid ground in reasoning that no commander in the field had a right to issue such a sweeping declaration. It was the president, with a broad view of the military and political landscape, who must make such decisions. Lincoln, who had said that he would like to have God on his side but must have Kentucky, modified Frémont's proclamation, making it conform to the First Confiscation Act, saying that, as it had been issued, it would "alarm our Southern Union friends and turn them against us; perhaps ruin our rather fair prospect for Kentucky."

A year later, Lincoln's friend David Hunter became the second general so to act. After the Sea Islands of South Carolina, Georgia, and Florida had been occupied by Union troops, Hunter had been made commander of the Union forces in the islands. As such, he declared that all slaves in the three states were "forever free." When Lincoln slapped down Hunter's proclamation, the reaction of black people to what they thought of as a second outrage against freedom was at least as bitter as it had been to the first. Phillip Bell, editor of the *Pacific Appeal*, wrote that slavery was still standing "to branch forth again and diffuse its malignant and pestiferous poison over the land."

As Lincoln suffered over Willie's death, as he agonized over military losses, and resisted pressure from the abolitionists, he worried almost constantly about what would happen to freed slaves. If a people who had purposely been barred from education stayed in North America, how long would it be before they could clothe and house and feed themselves? Until they could, who would teach them and take care of them? Lincoln hadn't had much luck in persuading many black Americans to colonize, but he clung desperately to the notion that he would one day be successful.

The question of what to do with fugitives from slavery became ever more insistent as slaves left their masters and came into Union lines, hoping they would be allowed to fight or, in some way, help to bring about a victory. These people were called "contrabands." The term was coined by Massachusetts General Benjamin Butler, a rotund, balding, red-faced man who was more a lawyer than a soldier. In the spring of 1861, Butler, in command of Fortress Monroe—a Union stronghold on the coast of Virginia—raised an underlying question: In a war started over slavery, could the Union give support, direct or otherwise, to slaveholders? Clearly not. Butler found a way to demonstrate his argument. One dark night, three fugitives were admitted to the fort. These men had been used to erect Confederate earthworks. Flying in the face of Lincoln's purpose at that stage of the war—to return slaves to their owners—Butler reasoned that, since the three men were believed by their owners to be property and had been used for military purposes, they were contraband of war, as surely as were captured cannon, ammunition, food, wagons, or entrenching tools, and he put them to work for him. The news of Butler's action spread throughout the vast community of slaves and what had been a trickle of contrabands became a flood, not only at Fortress Monroe, but at other Union barracks and encampments, too.

Slaves who came into Union territory were considered contraband of war and accordingly called "contrabands." *National Archives*

Most contrabands, like the black men in this photograph, worked behind the Union lines. Many served in Union regiments. *National Archives*

In the spring of 1862, as Lincoln started working on the Emancipation Proclamation, Congress passed more progressive legislation. New laws were enacted to prevent continuance of the slave trade and to outlaw slavery in the territories. Lincoln must have taken satisfaction from the passage of a law forbidding slavery in the District of Columbia—a measure he had been considering since 1837. In a letter to Charles Sumner, Frederick Douglass wrote, "I trust I am not dreaming, but the events taking place seem like a dream."

In the midst of celebration in the District of Columbia, another man who had been born a slave asked, "Should I not feel glad to see so much rejoicing around me? Were I a drinker I would get on a Jolly spree today." As it was, the man was content to kneel and pray and bless God for his freedom.

On July 17, Congress passed another Confiscation Act, declaring that all slaves of rebel masters were "forever free," but this act lacked the broad implications of Lincoln's Preliminary Proclamation to be published two months later.

Aside from military failures, the question of what to do with contrabands was perhaps the president's greatest worry. Sometimes, when people talked to him about it, his face took on a strained and tortured look. As the unexpected flood of contrabands increased, he returned repeatedly to the notion that America's free black people, as well as contrabands, might establish democratic governments outside the United States.

The American Colonization Society—whose efforts had spanned forty years—had encouraged emigration by black people to Liberia, where it had bought coastal lands. As we have seen, some black Americans had gone to Liberia. The experiment had been largely unsuccessful but many people still believed—as did Lincoln at that stage—that black people and white people couldn't live and work together. White people stationed just above black people on the economic scale were afraid of competition from black laborers. Resentment, mostly among Irish immigrants who themselves had been the target of discrimination, had already brought about distressing demonstrations and was soon to generate the most vicious riot in the history of New York.

Most black leaders were outraged at the thought of colonization. Douglass was one of these. He said that "the place for the free colored people is the land where their brothers and sisters are held in slavery, and where circumstances might some day enable them to contribute an important part to their liberation." Others, facing an eternity of hatred, violence, and suppression, were in favor of abandoning their country to a people who had never given them a chance to prove their worth.

On July 22, Lincoln read the first draft of his proclamation to the members of his cabinet and, less than a month later, asked a delegation of representative black men—as distinguished from black leaders—to come to his office in the White House. In conversation with his visitors, he spoke again of the need for segregation of the races. He suggested that black people colonize in large numbers. His manner was both kind and gentle. However, what he said was condescending: "You and we are different races," he informed them. "It is better for us both, therefore, to be separated."

Black journalists expressed their outrage at the president's behavior. Abolitionists, both black and white, scorned his attitude and his proposal. One black journalist suggested, "How much better would be a manly protest against prejudice and a wise effort to give freemen homes in America!"

In spite of the failure in Liberia, Lincoln gave his support to a plan involving emigration to Chiriquí, what is now Barú, Panama. Under the auspices of the Chiriquí Improvement Company, free black Americans and contrabands could work coal mines in Chiriquí, but promoters of the plan turned out to be corrupt, and Lincoln backed off just in time to avoid what would have been a conspicuous disaster. In most matters, he was capable of learning from experience, but he learned nothing from Liberia or Chiriquí. He already had another emigration project up his sleeve.

Neither Lincoln nor his secretaries could read all the criticism heaped on him during 1862, but Lincoln did pay attention to the sometimes highly negative comments of Horace Greeley—the antislavery founder and editor of the

New York *Tribune.* In an open letter to the president—titled "The Prayer of Twenty Millions" and published on August 20—Greeley faulted Lincoln for repeatedly conciliating slaveholders.

In his reply, sent on August 22, Lincoln said in part,

> My paramount object in this struggle *is* to save the Union and is *not* either to save or to destroy slavery. If I could save the Union without freeing any slave, I would do it; and if I could save it by freeing all the slaves, I would do it; and if I could save it by freeing some and leaving others alone, I would also do that. What I do about slavery, and the colored race, I do because I believe it helps to save the Union.

He left no doubt in anybody's mind that this was his *official* view, that his feelings about slavery itself remained unchanged. "I intend no modification of my oft-expressed *personal* wish that all men every where could be free."

Lincoln's final serious attempt to colonize Americans involved emigration to Isle à Vache—Cow Island—off the south coast of Haiti. The Chiriquí project had been canceled before anyone was hurt. Not so in the case of the Isle à Vache adventure, in which 453 black volunteers were transported to the island to cut timber or to give support to those who did.

Throughout Lincoln's presidency, his secretaries John G. Nicolay and John Hay were with him almost constantly. This is an engraving from a photograph by Alexander Gardner, taken on November 8, 1863. About the photograph, John Hay wrote in his diary, "Nico & I immortalized ourselves by having ourselves done in a group with the President." *Williams College Sawyer Library*

If the promoters of Chiriquí were unscrupulous, the behavior of the men who hoped to profit from the sale of timber harvest on Isle à Vache was criminal. Some emigrants slept on the ground. Other slept in flimsy huts. Close to one hundred died of smallpox or starvation. At last, as news of the disaster spread, Congress cut off the flow of funds to the project, and Lincoln sent a ship to rescue the remaining emigrants.

Wartime attempts to colonize black people had begun on a sunny, happy note. A poem that appeared on June 22, 1861, in *Pine and Palm*—a newspaper edited and published by black crusaders to promote emigration to the tropics—expressed the kind of optimism felt by people who had believed in emigration.

> *Ho! children of the dusky brow!*
> *Why will ye wear the chain?*
> *A fairer home is waiting you,*
> *In isles beyond the main!*

Exploitation and corruption had destroyed attempts to colonize but, in any circumstances, emigration would have failed. Most free black Americans didn't want to leave their native land. The best thing that can be said about Lincoln's effort to persuade black Americans to colonize is that it remained an effort to *persuade*. Lincoln never, ever, recommended anything but voluntary emigration. The policies of other, later, wartime presidents in dealing with minorities were less enlightened, less humane.

Three months after the Battle of Antietam and on the eve of Lincoln's issuance of the final version of the Emancipation Proclamation, Union soldiers under General Ambrose Burnside, who were heading toward the Confederate capital at Richmond, suffered a humiliating loss in Fredericksburg—a Virginia river town, settled in 1671. In the maneuvering that preceded the conflict, Robert E. Lee took up an impregnable position on Marye's Heights, overlooking the brown waters of the Rappahannock. Burnside foolishly launched a series of attacks on Lee, in which he gained nothing, lost at least 12,000 men, and retreated.

As the extent of the failure dawned on the administration, Lincoln and his advisors came in for a hail of criticism. Burnside willingly took the blame, but members of Lincoln's cabinet blamed one another for the failure. Seward was prepared to resign, but Lincoln, who stayed calm throughout the storm, kept his cabinet as it was.

There had always been at least a shadow of a doubt in some

Confederate dead, at Fredericksburg, following the defeat of Union soldiers on Marye's Heights. The failure brought on quarrels among members of the Lincoln cabinet but the president kept them in place and stayed calm throughout the storm. *National Archives*

quarters as to whether Lincoln would, in fact, ever issue an emancipation proclamation. The defeat at Fredericksburg heightened speculation over Lincoln's resolution, but he seldom broke a promise and, once determined, held his course.

At a cabinet meeting on Tuesday, December 30, he distributed printed copies of the Emancipation Proclamation. Several cabinet members made suggestions, as they did again on Wednesday. He worked past midnight on the document, while in churches in the North people prayed that it would indeed be issued New Year's Day. It was.

In its first important paragraph, the edict stated, "That on the first day of January, A.D. 1863, all persons held as slaves within any State or designated part of a State the people whereof shall then be in rebellion against the United States shall be then, thenceforward, and forever free."

Freed slaves, seen here in the Sea Islands of South Carolina, were employed to harvest and sort cotton, which was then shipped to textile factories, most of which were in New England. Lincoln's friend David Hunter was, at first, commander of the Union forces in the islands but apparently had no control over Northern cotton brokers, some of whom were corrupt and profited from the labor of freed slaves. Other people from the North taught freed people how to grow things for themselves and taught them to read and write. *U.S. Army Military History Institute*

This provision changed the purpose of the Civil War. On the first day of January, Union soldiers found themselves fighting for the freedom of four million slaves. Some critics thought that the document lacked moral force; others saw it as a purely military measure. Frederick Douglass, in no mood to quibble, said of it, "I hail it as the doom of slavery in all the States. I hail it as the end of all that miserable statesmanship, which has for sixty years juggled and deceived the people by professing to reconcile what is irreconcilable."

Though there were those who doubted the effectiveness of Lincoln's proclamation, nobody failed to recognize its clear invitation to black men to join the fight to save the Union and so do away with slavery. "And I further declare and make known that such persons of suitable condition will be received into the armed service of the United States to garrison forts, positions, stations, and other places, and to man vessels of all sorts in said service." Thanks to this provision of the proclamation, 200,000 black Americans—in the Union Army and Navy—were soon to engage in an enduring struggle, not only for the liberation of their brothers, but for respect and for equality.

Lincoln's Emancipation Proclamation brought great joy to black people everywhere. On a South Carolina island occupied by Union forces, Charlotte Forten, a free black woman from Philadelphia who had come to teach the Sea Island children, listened as a local minister read every word of Lincoln's document. Forten described the scene: "There were the black soldiers, in their blue coats and scarlet pants, and the officers of this and other regiments in their handsome uniforms, and some crowds of onlookers, men, women and children, grouped in various attitudes, under the trees. Their faces wore a happy, eager, expectant look."

Robert Sutton—a tall noncommissioned officer soon to become a hero—made what Forten thought was a touching and impressive speech, after which two regiments of contrabands marched past the reviewing stand. "The dress parade—the first I have ever seen—delighted me. It was a brilliant sight—the long line of men in their bright uniforms, with bayonets gleaming in the sunlight."

In Washington, free black minister Henry Turner grabbed the last remaining tattered copy of *The Evening Star*, which contained the final text of

A direct result of issuance of the Emancipation Proclamation was recruitment of the first black regiment raised in the North. *The collection of the author*

the proclamation. The minister, chased by people who had been denied a copy, ran down Pennsylvania Avenue. He remembered:

> When the people saw me coming with the paper in my hand they raised a shouting cheer that was almost deafening. As many as could get around me lifted me to a great platform, and I started to read the proclamation. I had run the best end of a mile, I was out of breath and could not read. Mr. Hinton, to whom I handed the paper, read it with great force and clearness. . . . Men squealed, women fainted, dogs barked, white and colored people shook hands, songs were sung, and by this time cannons began to fire at the navy yard, and follow in the wake of the roar that had for some time been going on behind the White House. . . . Great processions of colored and white men marched to and fro and congratulated President Lincoln on his proclamation. . . . It was indeed a time of times, and a half time, nothing like it will ever be seen again in this life.

★ 10 ★

THE WORLD WILL LITTLE NOTE

On the eve of Lincoln's trip to Gettysburg, Pennsylvania, where he planned to speak briefly at the dedication of a military cemetery, he might well have hesitated to abandon the White House. His son Tad was gravely ill. His wife Mary, thinking Tad might follow his dead brothers, was distracted and hysterical.

Lincoln might have hesitated, but he had important things to say and thought that they had best be said near the hills, ravines, and valleys of the rural Pennsylvania town where, four months or so before, more than 40,000 young Americans had died or had been wounded in a three-day battle.

Where timing was concerned, Lincoln listened only to himself. This was never more apparent than in the days before he left for Gettysburg. Secretary of War Stanton had at first planned the presidential journey so that Lincoln would arrive just in time to be present at the ceremonies, which would feature an oration by Edward Everett, a long speech to be followed by what were supposed to be "a few appropriate remarks by the President of the United States." But, in an age when trains broke down often and schedules were disrupted by the need to

Lincoln photographed by Matthew Brady, less than two months after he spoke at The Soldiers' National Cemetery, at Gettysburg, Pennsylvania. During the Civil War, Brady took distinguished photographs of living soldiers and heartbreaking photographs of the aftermath of battles. *National Archives*

carry men and weapons to war zones, Lincoln wasn't willing to risk missing the occasion altogether. He told Stanton, "I do not like this arrangement. I do not wish to so go that by the slightest accident we fail entirely. . . ."

The presidential train left Washington at noon on November 18, 1863—the day before the ceremony. Because it was necessary for Lincoln's crowded railway car to be ventilated, several windows were ajar. Soot sifted in, bringing with it the familiar acrid smell of incinerated coal. Laughter and the sounds of animated conversation filled the air. A steam whistle shrieked at every overpass and crossing.

Much nonsense has been published about Lincoln's writing of the Gettysburg Address. The most unlikely story of them all has him scratching out the speech on the back of a tattered envelope. Years later, a friend and associate, hoping he might share a fragment of the veneration Lincoln brought upon himself as he delivered the address, said he saw the president writing and revising it en route to Gettysburg. But, knowing Lincoln as a man who thought deeply and deliberately about every word he wrote, most responsible historians ignore accounts of the easy composition of his masterpiece.

On the train, he was interrupted constantly by friends, cabinet members, and his secretaries, Nicolay and Hay. He had little time for writing, much less for meditation. He probably wrote several drafts of the address in the White House. He finished it in Gettysburg. We know this because Nicolay reported joining him in his room on the morning of the ceremony and remaining with him while he made last-minute changes in it; but Nicolay claimed no credit for the wording of the Gettysburg Address.

Lincoln and his entourage changed cars in Baltimore, where the first bloodshed of the war had taken place—a dangerous city for an antislavery president. In Baltimore, more friends and several local politicians joined the presidential party. After one more change of cars, at Hanover Junction, Lincoln's train clanged and rattled into Gettysburg at dusk.

As he stepped down from his railway car, Lincoln saw that empty caskets had been stacked on the platform. These were destined to contain what remained of the bodies of young soldiers soon to be taken from their temporary graves on the surrounding battlefields and given formal burial in a new cemetery. Lincoln's host, David Wills, and Edward Everett greeted him. Wills—a thirty-two-year-old lawyer, banker, and leading citizen—was acting for Pennsylvania Governor Andrew Curtin in organizing the reburial of soldiers and the dedication ceremonies. Everett, who was sixty-nine, had been a preacher, legislator, foreign minister, and college president.

As Wills walked with Lincoln to his house on the town square, the streets and alleyways of Gettysburg were in shadow—a dusk broken here and there by lamplight in a parlor or a kitchen. Lincoln's white shirtfront, his swarthy skin, and his dark beard were common features in the 1860s, but his extraordinary height and his penetrating voice made him conspicuous, and he was recognized by many of the visitors who had gathered to pay tribute to the fallen warriors.

After supper, a crowd led by a military band gathered under Lincoln's bedroom window. When the band finished playing, someone shouted to the president, asking him to make a speech. He went downstairs, stood on the porch, and raised his hand: "I appear before you fellow citizens, merely to thank you for this compliment. The inference is a very fair one that you would hear me, for a little while at least, were I to commence to make a speech. I do not appear before you for the purpose of doing so, and for several substantial reasons." Not wanting to elaborate, he said simply, "The most substantial of these is that I have no speech to make. In my position it is somewhat important that I should not say any foolish things."

Someone in the crowd called out, "If you can help it!"

Lincoln must have smiled as he answered, "It very often happens that the only way to help it is to say nothing at all."

Shortly after dawn the next morning, Lincoln went with Secretary of State

Dead rifleman in a ravine at Gettysburg. *National Archives*

William H. Seward in a carriage to the places where the three-day battle had been fought. They stepped down to walk awhile. Lincoln, who still wore a mourning band on his hat for Willie, must have thought about the people who had lost their sons on that Pennsylvania killing ground. He and Seward viewed the patches of scorched earth, overlaid with whitened bones, where the carcasses of mules and horses had been burned. He saw partly buried skeletons of soldiers, wrapped in threadbare uniforms, their pockets long since picked by scavengers who had walked across the battlefields, brushed away bluebottle flies, and gathered souvenirs. Some were buried under crude wooden crosses. Most lay in unmarked graves.

Lincoln was in Gettysburg to give meaning to a butchery, to say something to ennoble thousands of Americans—many of them little more than children—who had perished in a battle that had given neither side a decisive military victory but had forced General Lee to retreat to the flooded northern banks of the Potomac with the sense of a lost cause, a cause he would doggedly pursue for twenty months, during which thousands more young soldiers would be killed and whole cities in America's Southland would be shelled and burned and left in desolation.

Having little to be proud of, Lee had offered to resign, and General George G. Meade, in command of exhausted Union soldiers, had offered to relinquish his command because he hadn't hounded Lee's half-starved, footsore, and discouraged men. Another chance to end the war had slipped through the fingers of a Union general. In fact, Lincoln was so frustrated over Meade's performance—which had almost paralleled McClellan's ten months earlier—that he had written him a stinging letter but had had the good sense not to send it.

Americans were sick of war. Especially tired of it were the residents of certain towns in Virginia, Maryland, Pennsylvania, and especially Mississippi—where Confederate soldiers and civilians at Vicksburg, long under siege, had surrendered on July 4, to General Ulysses S. Grant, whose aggressive tactics were soon to prompt Lincoln to make him commander of all Union armies.

This kind of war was a far cry from the first Battle of Bull Run at Manassas

Junction, where on a summer's day men and women, dressed for play, had come out with picnic baskets to observe the fighting. These later battles had disrupted people's lives. The bodies of dead soldiers and dead animals had littered country roads and wooded hills in and near the towns of Fredericksburg, Sharpsburg, and Gettysburg. People suffered in the siege of Vicksburg, where civilians stole food from one another, where beleaguered soldiers pilfered animals and plucked produce from the gardens of already starving families, where chicken was a rarity and mule meat began to taste like beef. Telegraph lines lay in segments, and mail service was a distant memory. Rumor took the place of news. Isolation threatened to drive people mad.

Worse than any other hardship of the war was the grief of parents who had lost their sons. The father of a boy who fell at Gettysburg was reported to have told David Wills or one of his subordinates, "I have come to take back my son's body, for his mother's heart is breaking and she will not be satisfied until it is brought home to her."

In Gettysburg, in the town square, visible from Lincoln's window, more than a hundred saddle horses, tended by as many stableboys, awaited dignitaries who would lead the procession to the cemetery.

At ten o'clock, Lincoln went downstairs to take the mount assigned to him. The sky was bright. The soldiers wore blue uniforms, decorated with their service medals. The marshals organizing the procession wore red, white, and blue rosettes on their chests. The white silk saddlecloths were edged in black.

Some accounts have Lincoln on a horse too small for him, but a young man named Clark E. Carr, whose chronicle of the occasion seems a careful, honest one, says no such thing. Apparently, Lincoln rode a horse that suited him. A good horseman, he was comfortable and confident. He was at first both erect and dignified, but as he rode along the dusty country road leading to the cemetery, his white gauntlets resting lightly on his reins, he seemed withdrawn, absorbed in thought.

> Before he reached the grounds he was bent forward, his arms swinging,
> his body limp, and his whole frame swaying from side to side . . . and he

Union steamboats landing soldiers and supplies north of Vicksburg. Grant's assaults on the city failed to penetrate its defenses but he and his soldiers crossed the Mississippi south of the city and were able to cut off its supply of food and ammunition, forcing it to surrender. Grant's success led to control of the Mississippi River. *National Archives*

was riding just as he did over the circuit in Illinois, during the years of his early practice of the law, with his saddle bags, which contained all of his possessions, dangling upon each side of the horse.

About 15,000 people gathered at the cemetery. Following two intervals of military music and a prayer, Everett moved up to the lectern and put down his manuscript. His hair was white. He was tall, though not as tall as Lincoln. He was a seasoned orator, who used his gestures and his voice to good effect.

Everett talked for two full hours, never looking at the written version of his text. In an age when debates, plays, recitations, and orations were happily anticipated entertainments, his speech was an unqualified success. His ac-

A family of white Confederate refugees prepared to flee from advancing Union soldiers. *National Archives*

count of the battle, based on thorough scholarship, including interviews with men who had been commanders in the field, was the first to appear in any form.

He started on a modest and poetic note: "Standing beneath this serene sky, overlooking these broad fields now reposing from the labors of the waning year, the mighty Alleghenies dimly towering before us, the graves of our brethren beneath our feet, it is with hesitation that I raise my poor voice to break the eloquent silence of God and Nature."

He spoke at length about the politicians and the warriors of ancient Greece, about Pericles, who in 430 B.C. gave a speech over ashes of Athenians killed in battle, a speech in which he called upon the patriotic feelings of the citizens of his ruined and defeated city. Everett took his listeners through the standing history of the Civil War, and in so doing, set the stage for Gettysburg. He described the pulse of conflict, weakening at sundown of the first day and reviving on two fateful mornings. Everett then placed the blame for all the carnage, sorrow, and despair on slaveholders, on the "hard-hearted men whose cruel lust of power brought this desolating war upon the land." It was a crime, he said, to have rebelled against the federal government. Then, expressing optimism, he predicted that the bitterness of war would not prevent a restoration of the Union. He bestowed a "benediction on these honored graves."

He predicted something that in a later, less romantic age would become impossible. He said that wherever history was read, "there will be no brighter page than that which relates to the Battle of Gettysburg."

Lincoln, Nicolay, and Hay, who had read only brief and fragmentary summaries of the battle, pieced together from dispatches, thought the speech was masterful. They joined wholeheartedly in the applause.

Carr remembered, "At the close of Mr. Everett's address a solemn dirge . . . was sung by a hundred voices, after which President Lincoln was introduced to the great multitude."

When Lincoln rose, there was confusion in the crowd around him, as spectators pushed and elbowed neighbors so that they could catch a glimpse of him. He stood quietly, head bowed slightly, putting on his spectacles, waiting for the audience to settle down. Carr, who sat close to him, said that he had never seen "any other human being who was so stately, and majestic." Lincoln's gentle face "had a sad, mournful, almost haggard, and still hopeful expression."

Had Lincoln been a baritone, his words would have reached only people close to him. As it was, his tenor voice had a penetrating quality. He began, "Four score and seven years ago our fathers brought forth on this continent, a new nation, conceived in Liberty, and dedicated to the proposition that all men are created equal." Thomas Jefferson's Declaration of Independence had proclaimed ". . . that all men are created equal, that they are endowed by their Creator with certain inalienable Rights, that among these are Life, Liberty and the pursuit of Happiness."

Though there was nothing new in the notion that all people are or should be equal under law, Lincoln's words dusted off the document that had prompted ragged bands of patriots to go to war against the tidy ranks of smartly uniformed redcoats eighty-seven years before. Not mentioning North or South, or slavery or freedom, Lincoln posed a clear choice between acceptance of the letter and the spirit of the Declaration and the continuance of slavery. Lincoln had, long since, made the choice for himself, as he had demonstrated many times in his argument with Stephen Douglas. Lincoln was pointing out that it was time, or that it would soon be time, for all Americans to make that choice. At Gettysburg, he made the people see the Declaration in a bright new light: as founding law.

> Now we are engaged in a great civil war, testing whether that nation, or any nation so conceived and so dedicated, can long endure. We are met on a great battle-field of that war. We have come to dedicate a portion of that field, as a final resting place for those who here gave their lives that that nation might live. It is altogether fitting and proper that we should do this.

Here, Lincoln made no distinction between soldiers from the North and soldiers from the South. He had never recognized the government of the Confederacy. To him, the Civil War was the disruption of a single government, a dangerous hitch in a continuing experiment entered into by a single people. In Lincoln's view, a young man from Georgia or from Texas was as much a part of the experiment—testing whether true democracy could live and flourish—as was a New Yorker or New Englander.

Lincoln continued:

> But, in a larger sense, we can not dedicate—we can not consecrate— we can not hallow—this ground. The brave men, living and dead, who struggled here have consecrated it, far above our poor power to add or detract. The world will little note, nor long remember what

we say here, but it can never forget what they did here. It is for us the living, rather, to be dedicated here to the unfinished work which they who fought here have thus far so nobly advanced. It is rather for us to be here dedicated to the great task remaining before us—that from these honored dead we take increased devotion to that cause for which they gave the last full measure of devotion—that we here highly resolve that these dead shall not have died in vain—that this nation, under God, shall have a new birth of freedom—and that government of the people, by the people, for the people, shall not perish from the earth.

Carr remembered that the president delivered most of his address in a strong voice but that he revealed emotion as he said, "The world will little note, nor long remember. . . ." It is impossible to say why he so hesitated, but there is no question that he was looking far beyond his own life span. He was predicting that, following a Union victory, there would be reconciliation and renewed dedication to democracy. He was optimistic, but he may have guessed that it would be at least one hundred years before reconciliation was complete. He may have known that it might take twice that long before the bitter fruit of slavery would begin to wither on the vine.

Why was the Gettysburg Address a work of genius, comparable to what was said more than two thousand years before by Pericles? At Gettysburg, in language spare and classical, not only did Lincoln call attention to the Declaration of Independence, a document that had been willfully ignored, but he forced Americans to reevaluate their Constitution, which, without amendments added later, was a shameful document. In his address, Lincoln gave voice to his insistent belief that slavery, if allowed to flourish, would destroy democracy. He reaffirmed his belief that Americans were destined to give freedom to themselves and to the people of the world.

On July 4, 1854, William Lloyd Garrison, who had called the Constitu-

Address delivered at the dedication of the
Cemetery at Gettysburg.

Four score and seven years ago our fathers
brought forth on this continent, a new nation, conceived in Liberty, and dedicated
to the proposition that all men are created equal.

Now we are engaged in a great civil war,
testing whether that nation, or any nation
so conceived and so dedicated, can long
endure. We are met on a great battle field
of that war. We have come to dedicate a
portion of that field, as a final resting
place for those who here gave their lives
that that nation might live. It is altogether fitting and proper that we should
do this.

But, in a larger sense, we can not dedicate— we can not consecrate— we can not
hallow— this ground. The brave men, living and dead, who struggled here have con-
secrated it, far above our poor power to add
or detract. The world will little note, nor

long remember what we say here, but it can never forget what they did here. It is for us the living, rather, to be dedicated here to the unfinished work which they who fought here have thus far so nobly advanced. It is rather for us to be here dedicated to the great task remaining before us — that from these honored dead we take increased devotion to that cause for which they gave the last full measure of devotion — that we here highly resolve that these dead shall not have died in vain — that this nation, under God, shall have a new birth of freedom — and that government of the people, by the people, for the people, shall not perish from the earth.

Abraham Lincoln.

November 19, 1863.

A copy of Lincoln's Gettysburg Address, made by him for the Soldier's and Sailor's Fair, held in Baltimore, Maryland, on November 8, 1864. *Williams College Sawyer Library*

tion "a covenant with death and an agreement with hell," had staged a public burning of a copy of the document. At Gettysburg, nine years later, Lincoln's language and his gestures were more moderate than Garrison's, but recognizing that the founding fathers tragically had failed to come to terms with slavery, he reinterpreted the Constitution. In so doing, he prepared his countrymen for amendments yet to come.

Reaction to the Gettysburg Address was mixed. Some saw it as commonplace. Others comprehended its wide significance. An editor of the Chicago *Times*, who understood and disliked its message, told his readers that, in his address, the president had ignored the Constitution:

> It was to uphold this Constitution, and the Union created by it, that our officers and soldiers gave their lives at Gettysburg. How dared he, then, standing on their graves, mistake the cause for which they died, and libel the statesmen who founded the government? They were men possessing too much self-respect to declare that negroes were their equals, or were entitled to equal privileges.

Most Americans were slow to recognize the significance of the Gettysburg Address. Several British journalists were quick to do so. London's *Spectator* and *Saturday Review* published highly favorable comments. The *Edinburgh Review* proclaimed that no other speech, except that of Pericles made in eulogy of the heroes of the Peloponnesian War, could begin to measure up to it.

Lincoln returned from Gettysburg to find that Tad had recovered from his illness but he was himself feeling shaky and discovered that he had a fever brought on by what was probably a weak variant of smallpox. He was a self-effacing man and so failed to realize how surpassing a speech he had made at Gettysburg; but, even as he took to the presidential bed, he was in good spirits. One day, during his three weeks in quarantine, thinking of the many people who were asking him for favors, he told John Hay, "Now I have something I can give everybody."

Mild illnesses often give reflective people time to map the work that lies ahead of them. Lincoln welcomed such an opportunity. First, he must end the war. Then, in a message soon to be delivered to the Congress, he would begin to wrestle with the issue of restoring to an angry Southern people what he thought of as their rightful place in the Union. As he lay three weeks in bed, he began to concentrate on his plans for Reconstruction.

★ 11 ★

GET DOWN, YOU FOOL

A year after Lee led the ragged remnants of his army south from Gettsysburg, Washington was still in danger. On July 2, 1864, Union scouts saw an army of Confederate soldiers marching north in the Shenandoah Valley. General Grant, dug in in front of Richmond, had left the capital only lightly garrisoned.

Telegraph lines between Washington and Harpers Ferry had gone dead, but it wasn't long before bargemen navigating the canals and shallows northwest of the city brought the news that the fords of the Potomac swarmed with soldiers wearing light gray uniforms. The residents of the capital were frightened. Wounded veterans and civilians took up any weapons they could find and walked or rode out to the forts and bridges that surrounded Washington.

On July 11, Lincoln, knowing that the enemy was threatening Fort Stevens—not far from the White House—and finding it impossible to remain in his office waiting for dispatches that might never come, drove in his carriage to the fort, where the occupants were being fired on by Confederate riflemen. Fascinated by what was going on, Lincoln stood high on the rampart, with his tall hat on his head. Apparently unaware of how conspicuous he was, he peered through a borrowed telescope as Union troops marched out from the fort to chase away the attackers. A Union officer near him was hit and crumpled to the ground, causing twenty-three-year-old Captain Oliver Wendell Holmes to tell the president, "Get down, you fool, before you get shot!"*

Lincoln then watched from a safer perch until the Confederate soldiers turned and ran across open fields and hillocks to take cover in a wood. As Lincoln left to go back to the White House, he expressed both amusement and forgiveness, telling Holmes, "I'm glad to see that you know how to talk to a civilian."

The next day, when attacks were renewed, Lincoln went again to Fort Stevens, where he displayed continued disregard for his safety. But daring as he may have been at Fort Stevens, he had indulged in a kind of foolishness seen every day in his bravest and most skillful generals. In fact, Lincoln, who had at first been ignorant of military matters, had studied books on military strategies and had become an imaginative, sometimes intuitive, commander.

In 1861, the irrepressible Senator Charles Sumner, who was a close friend of Mary Lincoln and talked often to the president, had begun to urge Lincoln to employ black men in the war against the slave states. Toward the end of 1862, he had given him a copy of a paper by George A. Livermore. The paper, "An Historical Research Respecting the Opinions of the Founders of the Republic on Negroes as Slaves, as Citizens, and as Soldiers," had been read by Livermore to members of the Massachusetts Historical Society on August 14, 1862, and published later.

Using founding documents, Livermore—described by an acquaintance as "a merchant of even temper and moderate views"—presented arguments to prove that slavery had no lawful place in American democracy. Where slavery

*Young Holmes, whose father and namesake was a noted man of letters—poet, essayist, and biographer—was an associate justice of the U.S. Supreme Court from 1902 to 1932.

On November 7, 1861, referred to by former slaves as "the day of the big gun shoot," a fleet of Union warships sailed into Port Royal Sound. Thus began the Union occupation of the South Carolina coast. By 1862, many freed slaves were in uniform. Behind the soldiers in this photograph—taken in South Carolina—are an officer, two women teachers, and an older man who may be a teacher or a minister. *Library of Congress*

was concerned, Lincoln needed no persuasion, but Livermore's documented passages on black men as soldiers in the Revolutionary War had reinforced the president's maturing belief in the probable effectiveness of what Frederick Douglass called the nation's "powerful black arm."

In 1778, Colonel John Laurens, of South Carolina, had written to his father, who was president of the Continental Congress, "We have sunk the African and his descendants below the level of humanity." Laurens believed that service in the Continental Army would be a stepping-stone to true equality, "a proper gradation between abject slavery and perfect liberty."

In his paper, Livermore quoted part of a letter Laurens wrote to his friend George Washington, in which he lamented that the process of enlistment had been slowed by "a triple-headed monster, in which prejudice, avarice, and pusillanimity* were united."

Livermore wrote about the sacrifice of black patriot Crispus Attucks in the Boston Massacre, about the bravery of black patriots. He quoted one commander who had noted that on both sides in the Revolutionary War, there was "no regiment to be seen in which there were not negroes in abundance."

Black patriots had fought courageously at Lexington, Concord, Bunker Hill, Trenton, Brandywine, Monmouth, Yorktown, and elsewhere. They had fought in other, lesser, wars and, since Lincoln's issuance of the Emancipation Proclamation, had increasingly taken part in the struggle to defend the Union.

If anything changed Lincoln's view of the inherent qualities of black people, it was the loyalty and bravery of black men as they served in Union regi-

Pusillanimity is generally defined as timidity or cowardice.

Black men served in an unsegregated navy. *National Archives*

ments—none of whom had at first had the blessing or protection of the federal government. By the summer of 1863, he had seen abundant evidence that not only common laborers, but also prosperous black professionals would leave their families and fight and, if necessary, die for equality and freedom.

In Kansas, General James H. Lane—over protests from Secretary of War Stanton—had raised two regiments made up of fugitives from slavery. Lane and his men had fought in skirmishes with guerillas loyal to the South. They shed first blood in a battle on the Osage River, in Missouri, after which one rebel leader said that they had "fought like tigers."

Following the occupation of New Orleans, in the spring of 1862, General Benjamin Butler, in command of occupying forces, ignored Stanton, as had Lane, and took into federal service a militia unit called the "Louisiana Native Guards." This organization, which consisted of three regiments of black officers and men, had been organized before the war. As black participation in the war began, Francis E. Dumas, a soldier in the Native Guards, spoke not only for himself, but for others when he said, "No matter where I fight, I only wish to spend what I have, and fight as long as I can, if only my boy may stand in the street equal to a white boy when the war is over."

In the fall of 1862, General David Hunter—in command of an occupying army in the Sea Islands of South Carolina—called on Thomas Wentworth Higginson to take command of the First South Carolina Volunteers, a regiment of contrabands. Some members of this regiment had been drafted into service, but all performed efficiently, sometimes bravely, in attacks on the mainland. Higginson—who, in 1854, had been brave enough to storm Boston's Old Courthouse in an attempt to free fugitive slave Anthony Burns—had only praise for the bravery of his black enlisted men. He wrote, "Nobody knows anything about these men who has not seen them in battle. There is a fiery energy about them beyond anything of which I have ever read. . . . No officer in this regiment now doubts that the key to successful prosecution of this war lies in the unlimited employment of black troops."

Directly after issuance of the Emancipation Proclamation, General

Black soldiers standing in front of a South Carolina mansion, probably in Beaufort. The best houses on the Beaufort waterfront were occupied by former slaves and soldiers and missionaries from the North. *William Loren Katz collection*

Lorenzo Thomas began recruiting black men in the Mississippi valley. Six months later, the Washington *Daily Morning Chronicle* reported that Thomas had organized twenty black regiments in the lower Mississippi valley and done much to eradicate proslavery feeling "in all the armies of the West and South."

By the end of winter, most people in the North grudgingly approved of black participation in the military, but many still believed that black men—especially contrabands, most of whom had been downtrodden slaves—would cut and run at the first sound of cannon fire. The prevailing sentiment of white soldiers was summed up in a nasty little ditty:

> *In battle's wild commotion*
> *I won't at all object*

If a nigger should stop a bullet
Coming for me direct.

Black writer and historian William Wells Brown wrote about an episode that demonstrated the extraordinary bravery of the First Louisiana Regiment, part of the Native Guards. The regiment was made up of some of "the most wealthy and influential of the free colored people of New Orleans. One of its most efficient officers was Captain André Callioux, a man whose identity with his race could not be mistaken; for he prided himself on being the blackest man in Crescent City." Callioux, who had traveled widely and had lived in Paris, was a highly educated man and a strong and graceful athlete.

On the morning of May 26, 1863, the First Louisiana led a series of attacks on a Confederate stronghold at Port Hudson, on the Mississippi River. The defending batteries were on high ground and protected by a swamp. "Shells from rebel guns cut down trees three feet in diameter." One tree, Brown reported, buried a whole company underneath its branches.

In an attempt to take the stronghold, Callioux, in command of the leading

Headquarters, Second Brigade, Eighth Corps d'Afrique. This and other Union regiments fighting in Louisiana were composed of free black men and former slaves. The Eighth Corps d'Afrique was made up exclusively of former slaves and was commanded by Cyrus Hamlin, son of Lincoln's first vice president. *Massachusetts Historical Society*

company, was advancing under heavy fire. "Capt. Callioux was seen with his left arm dangling by his side—for a ball had broken it above the elbow—while his right hand held his unsheathed sword gleaming in the rays of the sun. . . . A moment more, and the brave and generous Callioux was struck by a shell, and fell far in advance of his company."

The assault was doomed to fail, but the soldiers of the Native Guards did not withdraw. A white observer wrote, "I can say for them that I never saw a braver company of men in my life." Not one of them fell back, until ordered to do so. "In fact, very few ever did fall back."

As General Thomas went to work in the Mississippi valley, Massachusetts Governor John A. Andrew—short, rotund, and energetic—asked Stanton for permission to raise several regiments of free black volunteers. As much as any wartime governor—with the possible exception of Lincoln's friend and protègè Richard Yates of Illinois—Andrew was a staunch defender of the Union and of Lincoln. Meeting Lincoln in Springfield after the Republican convention in Chicago, he had declared that the president-elect was "a pure, honest-minded, patriotic man, and whatever he did would be for the good of the country." He had seen "in a flash that here was a man who was master of himself."

On January 26, 1863, Stanton penned an order authorizing Andrew to recruit regiments of volunteers to be enlisted for three years. These units, Stanton wrote, "may include persons of African descent. . . ." Stanton promised to provide black regiments with "the proper transportation, organization, supplies, subsistence, arms and equipment. . . ." In his order, he said nothing about money. This omission was to lead to a long and bitter struggle over pay, during which Frederick Douglass was to talk to Lincoln.

It was determined that black regiments formed with the blessing of the federal government would, at first, be commanded by white officers, and Andrew lost no time in asking young and privileged Captain Robert Gould Shaw—who had fought at Antietam and elsewhere and had expressed an interest in black participation in the war—to command what became the first black regiment recruited in the North. The raising of what was known

Robert Gould Shaw, son of wealthy Northern abolitionists, was in command of the Fifty-Fourth Massachusetts regiment, whose enlisted men were black. Lincoln knew about the bravery of Shaw's men and, when some of them were captured, took steps to protect them. *Massachusetts Historical Society*

officially as the "Fifty-Fourth Regiment of Massachusetts Volunteer Infantry" released the pent-up energies of abolitionists, who began a widespread search, not only in the North, but in western states and Canada, for men of quality.

Frederick Douglass, who lived in Rochester, New York, where he had published a monthly abolitionist newspaper called *The North Star,* worked diligently to recruit men for the pioneering regiment. His first volunteer was his son Lewis, who was appointed sergeant major. His son Charles also joined the Fifty-Fourth but was sick when the regiment went off to war, so he was transferred to the Fifty-Fifth. Douglass also found a willing volunteer in James Caldwell, grandson of Sojourner Truth. Truth, a fearless agitator for the rights of her people, loved and was proud of her grandson and believed that enlistment of black soldiers was "the most hopeful feature of the war."

Following the training of the Fifty-Fourth, the regiment was sent to St. Helena—one of the Sea Islands of South Carolina—where Shaw established a base camp. For the most part, the men of the regiment lived up to expectations, as did their white officers; but before they had a chance to prove themselves in a battle, some were ordered to take part in a barbaric raid on a defenseless coastal village. The torching of Darien, Georgia, heralded the wholesale burning—a year later—of a string of Southern cities, towns, and villages by an all-white Union Army under General William Tecumseh Sherman.

However, Shaw and his men redeemed themselves when they attacked some of the defenses guarding Charleston. First, they fought gallantly on James

Island, where they rescued a white regiment—the Tenth Connecticut—from annihilation, then they attacked Fort Wagner, a huge Confederate earthwork that, together with more than a dozen other batteries, protected Charleston from amphibious attack.

With Shaw, waiting to attack Fort Wagner, was young Sergeant Robert Simmons, described by a white officer as "the finest-looking soldier in the Fifty Fourth, a brave man of good education."

Simmons wrote to his mother in New York, telling her about the bravery and the death of comrades on James Island: "God has protected me through this, my first fiery leaden trial, and I do give him the glory, and render praises unto His holy name." He finished with the words, "God bless you all! Goodbye! Likely we shall be engaged soon. Your affectionate son, R. J. Simmons."

On the evening of July 18, 1863—two weeks after Lee's withdrawal from

Lewis Douglass, son of Frederick Douglass, was sergeant major of the first black regiment recruited in the North. He fought bravely at Fort Wagner—an enormous earthwork guarding Charleston. *Moorland Spingarn Research Center, Howard University.*

Gettysburg—Shaw walked among his men, talking to them, giving them encouragement. An officer of his rank could have marched behind his men but he told them that he chose to lead the column.

As the sun hovered over Charleston and began to disappear behind the dunes, a mist settled on the sea. The sky was dark, the ocean sullen and forbidding. Small seabirds soared and cried above the cresting waves, as Union shells continued to explode above the fort.

Quiet followed the cessation of bombardment of the fort. Shaw and the leading elements of his command began to march. As they approached the walls of sand, earth, and palmetto logs, a Confederate officer, high on the southeast bastion, shouted to his riflemen and gunners. One of Shaw's officers, Captain Luis Emilio, remembered that "a sheet of flame, followed by a running fire, like electric sparks, swept along the parapet."

As Shaw moved, in double time, toward a moat fed by the waters of the sea, the sound of cannon fire boomed across the marshes, dunes, and beaches. Lieutenant Colonel Edward N. Hallowell remembered his last glimpse of his commander: "I saw him again, just for an instant, as he sprang into the ditch, his broken and shattered regiment were following him."

Sergeant Henry F. Stewart, called Harry, was a member of the Fifty-Fourth Massachusetts regiment. *Massachusetts Historical Society*

As Shaw crested the rampart, his men saw him etched against the deep night sky, then caught in a flash of cannon fire, as he crumpled and pitched headlong toward a cluster of Confederate gunners.

His men were at least as brave as Shaw. The color-bearer who had held the stars and stripes fell alongside his commander, but the others swarmed up the steep incline, leaped across the parapet, and engaged in hand-to-hand combat with the defenders. After an extended period of fighting, Lewis Douglass, shouting in a voice that echoed that of his distinguished father, tried to rally the exhausted men, but by then, it was clear that the fort could not be taken.

Dead black soldiers at Fort Wagner. This sketch, by Frank Vizetelly, was done the morning after the July 18, 1863 attack on the earthwork. *Courtesy of Harvard University*

Hallowell was wounded and was forced to retire, while Captain Emilio—the sole remaining officer—ordered that the regiment withdraw. Sergeant Carney, from New Bedford, Massachusetts, took up the tattered stars and stripes and, though he was wounded in three places, carried it back down the slope. Under fire, he struggled through a wasteland of dead soldiers, made his way to the rear, and stumbled into a large lamplit tent where the surgeons were at work.

Back on St. Helena, two days after the attack, Charlotte Forten, still teaching freed slave children, heard that a makeshift hospital in nearby Beaufort* was taking in men wounded at Fort Wagner, and she went to the hospital to distribute medicines, change bandages, and write letters for men wounded so severely that they couldn't hold a pencil or a pen.

---

*Harriet Tubman, hero of the Underground Railroad, then in her early forties, lived in Beaufort and was acting as a spy for the federal government. Tubman had repeatedly risked her freedom and her life to take fugitives to Canada. Widely publicized reports of her prewar activities had reinforced the arguments of abolitionists like Sumner who helped Lincoln find a way to follow the dictates of his own heart.

Forten had met Shaw several times, had had long talks with him, and called him a "much loved friend." She wrote in her diary,

> For nearly two weeks we have waited, oh how anxiously, for news of our regiment which went, we know, to Morris Island, to take part in the attack on Charleston. Tonight comes news, oh so sad, so heart sickening. It is too terrible, too terrible to write. . . . Colonel Shaw is killed and the regiment cut to pieces! I cannot, cannot believe it. And yet I know it may be so. But, oh, I am stunned, sick at heart. I can scarcely write. There was an attack on Fort Wagner. The Fifty Fourth, put in advance, fought bravely, desperately, but was finally over-powered and driven back, after getting into the fort. Thank heaven! They fought bravely!

Grieving over Shaw's death, Forten was especially touched by the courage of his men:

> After awhile, I went through the wards. As I passed along I thought, "Many and low are the pallets, but each is the face of a friend." And I was surprised to see such cheerful faces looking up from the beds. . . . One fellow here interests me greatly. He is very young, only nineteen, and comes from Michigan. He is badly wounded in both legs and there is a ball in his stomach—it is thought that cannot be extracted. This poor fellow suffers greatly. His groans are painful to hear. But he offers no complaint, and it is touching to see his gratitude for the least kindnesses that one does him.

To her astonishment, Forten discovered later that the young soldier had survived and gone home to Michigan. Forten wrote, "Brave fellows! I feel it a happiness, an honor, to do the slightest service for them."

Shaw's parents asked that their son's body not be moved from the trench where it had been buried with those of his fallen men. Hallowell recovered from his wound and took Shaw's place as colonel of the Fifty-Fourth. Sergeant Simmons, wounded and captured in the fort, was sent with sixty other men to Charleston and imprisoned in a dark and cheerless jail. Captain Emilio lived to write a history of the regiment. Sergeant Carney became the first black man to be awarded the Congressional Medal of Honor. Douglass survived to fight again.

Sergeant Simmons was transferred to the Old Marine Hospital, where his wounded arm became infected and—too late to save his life—was severed from his body. Mercifully, Simmons died unaware of what had happened to a member of his family in New York.

For four days—July 13 to 16—New York City was the scene of riots brought on partly by a provision of the Conscription Act of March 3, 1863, allowing men of military age to avoid being drafted by providing a fit substitute or by paying the federal government a fee of three hundred dollars. The people most affected by this law were Irish immigrants who could not afford to pay what, to them, was a large sum of money to avoid the draft. Some of these, enraged by the unfairness of the law, broke into an armory on Second Avenue, stole firearms and ammunition, and, so armed, had little trouble rounding up a mob that was large enough to overpower the militia and the police.

Harriet Tubman, as she looked in later life. Born in 1821, she died when she was in her 90's. *Massachusetts Historical Society*

Instead of taking out their anger on the legislators who had drafted the Conscription Act, the rioters concentrated on black people who, in many cases, were competing with them for employment. Rioters burned an orphanage that housed several hundred black children. They hung black men from lampposts, dragged their lifeless bodies through the streets.

On the third day of the riot, Simmons's sister left her two children with her mother, who lived in a tenement apartment on East Twenty-eighth Street. One was a babe in arms, and the other was a boy of seven, described as an attractive child and a good student who was tidy in his habits. He limped, but the cause and extent of his handicap is unknown.

When a mob swept into Simmons's mother's block, she tried to take the children to a place of safety but lost track of her elder grandchild. The rioters, finding him alone and helpless in the street, gave the boy a brutal beating. Bruised and stunned, he was rescued by a giant of a man named John McGovern, an off-duty fireman who carried him in his arms to the house of a German immigrant who nursed him, night and day, until his mother found him. She knelt by his bed and prayed, thanking God for restoring him to her, but her happiness was short-lived. The boy died some time later.

News of the riots found Lincoln at his wife's bedside, following a carriage accident in which her head had been injured. The president, aware that the riots had been sparked by the Conscription Act, had trouble justifying the act; but anxious as he was to win the war and needing soldiers for his armies, he refused to allow it to be challenged and revised. Moreover, he discouraged an investigation of the causes of the riots, believing that an inquiry would "touch a match to a barrel of gunpowder."*

Lincoln was deeply saddened by the news of the riots, by the terrible suffering of black people in New York. He was saddened by the justifiable uproar over the Conscription Act, but he continued to be buoyed by reports of the bravery of black soldiers as they fought to save the Union.

News of the extraordinary gallantry of the soldiers of the Fifty-Fourth reached Lincoln only hours after he had read reports of the riots in New York. The capture of black soldiers at Fort Wagner brought Lincoln face-to-face with a dilemma. The Confederate government had threatened to en-

---

*The causes of the riots were, in fact, investigated and recorded in the *Report of the Committee of Merchants for the Relief of Colored People Suffering from the Late Riots*, New York: G.A. Whitehorn, 1863.

slave or hang black soldiers captured in attacks on their positions. Contrabands were to be a special target, and a few of the soldiers taken at Fort Wagner had been slaves. Much as he hated threatening retailiation, Lincoln issued a stern proclamation signaling his determination to protect black prisoners of war.

EXECUTIVE MANSION, Washington, July 30, 1863

It is the duty of every government to give protection to its citizens of whatever class, color or condition, and especially to those who are duly organized as soldiers in the public service. The laws of nations and the usages and customs of war, as carried on by civilized powers, permit no distinction as to color in the treatment of prisoners of war as public enemies. To sell or enslave any captured person on account of his color, and for no offense against the laws of war, is a relapse into barbarism and a crime against the civilization of the age. The Government of the United States will give the same protection to all its soldiers; and if the enemy shall sell or enslave any one because of his color, the offense shall be punished by retaliation upon the enemy's prisoners in our hands.

It is therefore ordered that for every soldier of the United States killed in violation of the laws of war, a Rebel soldier shall be executed, and for every one enslaved by the enemy or sold into slavery, a Rebel soldier shall be placed at hard labor on the public works, and continue such labor until the other shall be released and receive the treatment due a prisoner of war.

Abraham Lincoln
By order of the Secretary of War,
E. D. Townsend, *Assistant Adjutant General*

Frederick Douglass first met Lincoln on August 10, 1863—less than a month after his son's regiment attacked Fort Wagner. Sumner and other Massachusetts abolitionists had urged the black leader to request an interview with Lincoln so that he could talk to him about matters that related to black participation in the military.

Douglass was in his mid-forties and still vigorous and youthful when he made his first trip to the White House. He had bright, compelling eyes. His shock of unruly hair was often likened to a lion's mane. A black beard extended his strong chin. He spoke forcefully but, like Lincoln, sometimes seemed indecisive. He had done the right thing in refusing to join John Brown in his suicidal raid on Harpers Ferry, but was never quite sure he had not been cowardly.

He had often criticized the president and believed that, at best, he might be greeted coldly. Such was not the case. He was escorted into Lincoln's presence with what he called

a modest estimate of my own consequence, and yet there I was to talk with, and even to advise, the head man of a great nation. Happily for me there was no vain pomp and ceremony about him. I was never more quickly or more completely put at ease in the presence of a great man than in that of Abraham Lincoln. He was seated when I entered, in a low arm-chair with his feet extended on the floor, surrounded by a large number of documents and several busy secretaries. The room bore the marks of business, and the persons in it, the President included, appeared to be much overworked and tired. Long lines of care were already deeply written on Mr. Lincoln's brow, and his strong face, full of earnestness, lighted up as soon as my name was mentioned. As I approached and was introduced to him he arose and extended his hand, and bade me welcome. I at once felt myself in the presence of an honest man—one whom I could love, honor and trust without reserve or doubt.

Douglass and the president were black and white, but the two had much in common. Both had taught themselves to read and write, and both had a firm command of language. Both had faced severity, sometimes cruelty, in child-hood, but both had been comforted by steadfast, loving women. Lincoln's wise and understanding stepmother had given him affection and encouragement, while the sympathetic, loving wife of a cruel master had been kind to Douglass. Once, in comforting the young slave, she had said, "Look up, child. Don't be afraid."

Douglass started to explain himself to Lincoln. "As I proceeded to tell him who I was and what I was doing, he promptly, but kindly, stopped me, saying, 'I know who you are, Mr. Douglass; Mr. Seward has told me all about you. Sit down. I am glad to see you.'"

Put at ease, Douglass lost little time in bringing up specific points. The black men of the Fifty-Fourth were paid less than white soldiers of the same rank. Douglass urged that the government grant black soldiers the same pay given their white counterparts. Though no black soldiers had yet been executed or mis-treated, Douglass next asked for swift retribution in such cases. Then he asked for prompt promotion for deserving black soldiers—recognition seldom given.

Provost Guard of the 107th Colored Infantry at Fort Corcoran, one of many forts and garrisons that protected Washington. *William Loren Katz collection*

"Mr. Lincoln listened with patience and silence to all I had to say. He was serious and even troubled by what I had said and by what he himself had evidently before thought upon the same points. He, by his silent listening not less than by his earnest reply to my words, impressed me with the solid gravity of his character."

In answer to the first point, Lincoln said that employment of black troops was a serious offense to what he called "popular prejudice." Because it was a great step forward, the willingness of black recruits to take less pay as the ex-

Most black soldiers serving in the Union armies had escaped from slavery. This young man exchanged his tattered clothes for a blue uniform and served as a Union drummer. Slaves of all ages left their masters so that they could fight for their freedom and the freedom of their brothers. *U.S. Army Military History Institute*

periment began was, he thought, a necessary sacrifice. No doubt thinking of resentment of white soldiers toward black competition, he said that, as black men proved themselves, their pay would be adjusted.

On the second point, Lincoln, who had just signed the order threatening "retaliation upon the enemy's prisoners in our hands," nonetheless expressed reluctance to carry out such a drastic policy and, in fact, never did so. He said that retaliation was a terrible remedy, that the thought of hanging any man for a crime done by someone else was "revolting to his feelings." Once started, where would such retaliation end? He added that he had information indicating "that colored soldiers were being treated as prisoners of war."

Sad to say, atrocities were yet to come.

Douglass tended to forgive the president for his stand on both issues: "In all this I saw the tender heart of the man rather than the stern warrior and commander-in-chief of the American army and navy, and, while I could not agree with him, I could but respect his humane spirit."

Lincoln had less trouble with the third point. He simply said that he would sign any commission to colored soldiers whom his Secretary of War should commend to him.

Douglass left the White House knowing he had made a friend.

Following the success of the first authorized black regiments, black men fought courageously in battles in most theaters of the Civil War. It was inevitable therefore that, despite Lincoln's promise of retaliation, atrocities would be committed by an outraged Southern soldiery. The worst of these occurred at Fort Pillow—an outpost on the Mississippi River—where a score of captured black soldiers and a few white officers were shot down in cold blood on April 13, 1864, the day after they surrendered. One of those who survived reported that a Confederate soldier shouted at him, "Damn you, what are you doing here?"

The black soldier looked his tormentor in the eye and said, "Please don't shoot me."

"Damn you, you are fighting against your master," his captor said, as he raised his gun and fired. The black soldier staggered and fell facedown in the mud.

An artist's version of the Fort Pillow massacre. Lincoln had threatened to retaliate for the killing or enslavement of black captured soldiers but, to him, the thought of hanging anyone for a crime done by someone else was "revolting to his feelings." *Massachusetts Historical Society*

It became common knowledge that young black men, some of them still in their teens, who were not in uniform and had worked as laborers had been shot by Confederate riflemen. After news of what had happened at Fort Pillow spread to the many thousands of black soldiers who had by then enlisted in black regiments, their battle cry became, "Remember Fort Pillow!"

★ 12 ★

AFTER LIFE'S FITFUL FEVER

On October 29, 1864, Sojourner Truth called on Lincoln.
A former slave, Truth was a living legend, widely known as an abolitionist and civil rights activist. Both religious and political, she was said to have dreaded passing through the Pearly Gates without having ever exercised her right to vote.

Truth didn't know, or wouldn't tell, how old she was. She expressed amusement when she said that, if people knew her age, it would, as she put it, "spoil my chances." She was well past middle age, but she had the energy and courage of a woman in her twenties. She was bright-eyed, thin, and sinewy and was fond of wearing white head-cloths, like those seen in parts of Africa.

In a letter to a friend, Truth described her visit to the president. As she waited in an anteroom, he appeared several times in a doorway and "showed as much kindness and consideration to the colored persons as to the whites—if there was any difference, more."

When she was taken in and introduced to Lincoln, he stood up, bowed, and said how pleased he was to see her. Truth, who had never questioned Lin-

Civil rights activist Sojourner Truth. Before and after she met Lincoln, she admired him and believed he was the best of all the presidents. *Massachusetts Historical Society*

coln's motives, told him that, when he had first taken office, she had been afraid he would be savaged, "for I likened you unto Daniel, who was thrown into the lions' den; and if the lions did not tear you to pieces, I knew that it would be God who had saved you; and I said if He spared me I would see you before the four years expired, and He has done so, and now I am here to see you for myself."

After Lincoln told her he was glad that she'd been spared, she said, "I appreciate you for you are the best President who has ever taken the seat."

Lincoln nodded, saying, "I expect you have reference to my having emancipated the slaves in my proclamation." He then mentioned several of his predecessors, giving special emphasis to George Washington. "They were all just as good, and would have done just the same if the time had come."

Lincoln then showed Truth an ornate leather-bound Bible, given to him by black citizens of Baltimore, and she reminded him of the many people who had been denied an education and had, therefore, been deprived of an opportunity to read the book.

She wrote later,

> I must say, and I am proud to say, that I never was treated with more kindness and cordiality than were shown me by that great and good man. . . . As I was taking my leave, he arose and took my hand, and said

he would be pleased to have me call again. I felt that I was in the presence of a friend, and I now thank God from the bottom of my heart that I have always advocated his cause, and have done so openly and boldly. I shall feel still more in duty bound to do so in time to come.

Black people by the millions, slave and free, had come to feel, as did Sojourner Truth, that Lincoln was especially sympathetic toward them. In return, most had given him unquestioning devotion. Though there remained in him some of the prejudices he had given voice to earlier, by the end of 1864, he had recognized the determination of most black Americans to stay in the United States; to defend the Union against hostile powers foreign and domestic; to agitate for their right to learn, to work, to vote, to themselves be defended; and to serve their countrymen in public office.

Poet and essayist Ralph Waldo Emerson once said, "Liberty is a slow fruit." In America, it was indeed slow to ripen, but the vines were strong and a beginning had been made.

Four months before, as Lincoln had risked his life on the rampart at Fort Stevens, his administration had been tottering. The uncertain progress of the war, the trouble over the Conscription Act, and, for some, black participation in the military—together with the determination of the Democrats to win back the power they had lost in 1860—were making trouble for Republicans in general and for Lincoln in particular.

After Lincoln had appointed Grant commander of all the armies of the

Ulysses S. Grant. Grant was a tough, aggressive general. He favored black participation in his armies. *National Archives*

United States—east and west, north and south—the general had come east to take charge of operations there, making his headquarters in Virginia.

Grant had welcomed the enlistment of black regiments in his armies. In a letter to the president, he had said, "I have given the subject of arming the negro my hearty support. This, with the emancipation of the negro, is the heaviest blow yet given the Confederacy. . . . By arming the negro we have added a powerful ally."

At the same time, Lincoln had addressed white soldiers, some of whom had had vicious things to say about black men in uniform and resented fighting in a war that had become a struggle to abolish slavery:

> You say you will not fight to free negroes. Some of them seem willing to fight for you. . . . There will be some black men who can remember that, with silent tongue, and clenched teeth, and steady eye, and well-poised bayonet, they have helped mankind to this great consummation; while, I fear there will be some white ones unable to forget that with malignant heart and deceitful speech, they strove to hinder it.

The lean, red-haired William Tecumseh Sherman, who took over Grant's command in the West, is an interesting study. Many people think of him as relentless, cold, and flinty. In making war, he was indeed relentless, as illustrated by his words: "To make war we must and will harden our hearts. . . . Know that war, like the thunderbolt, follows its laws and turns not aside even if the beautiful, the virtuous and charitable stand in its path." Yes, in making war, he was relentless, but he was more than a determined soldier. He was a cultivated man known for his charm and honesty. As did Lincoln, he read Shakespeare's plays and poetry.

Sherman's view of black soldiers was entirely different from that of his president. He minced no words: "I would prefer to have this a white man's war and provide for the negroes after the time has passed but we are in revolution and I must not pretend to judge." Despite the fact that black soldiers, who had been recruited by Lorenzo Thomas, had helped to pave the way for Sherman's capture of Atlanta and his march to Savannah, Sherman made a judgment that was unmistakable: "With my opinion of negroes and my experience, yea, prejudice, I cannot trust them yet."

Lincoln made no effort to persuade him to think otherwise. There were, therefore, no black soldiers in Sherman's army of 100,000 men—including cavalry—when he began the cruelest and the most effective operation of the war.

His march began in the spring of 1864 and took him along the railroad line from Chattanooga to Atlanta. As he moved south, he repeatedly outflanked his enemies and finally crossed the Chattahoochee River, northwest of Atlanta. Concentrating on encirclement, he sent forces to his right, where they severed railroad lines coming in from the South and the Southwest.

General John B. Hood, in command of the defending forces and facing a complete encirclement, was forced to order a retreat; and on September 1, after dark, the earth trembled and the sky was set aflame as his men blew up freight cars filled with ammunition that might better be destroyed than captured.

After Sherman occupied Atlanta, he gave orders to incinerate the city. His men went about the task with gusto, and by the time they were finished, most of Atlanta's anguished citizens had gone south and the city lay in ruins. Before the smoke had blown away, Sherman led his army toward the sea.

Remembering the high degree of bitterness generated by the burning of the town of Darien by black soldiers of the Fifty-Fourth and the coming need for all the peoples of America to work together during a

William Tecumseh Sherman was opposed to employing black men in his legions but was kind to the black people freed in his march from Atlanta to the sea. *National Archives*

long, cruel period of Reconstruction, it is fortunate that Sherman didn't take black soldiers with him as he waged his war against the South. Had thousands of black soldiers taken part in Sherman's march and in the looting and the burning of the cities of the South, the damage done to the reputations of black soldiers in particular, and to black Americans in general, might have been irreparable.

Sherman had used brutal tactics. It was not surprising, then, that black Southerners, as well as white, were frightened at the thought of an invasion by what seemed a foreign army. But the prospect of freedom—no more than a recurrent dream to people born in slavery—was irresistible.

Slaveholders who had loved their slaves, and expected them to want to stay with them, let it be known that they would continue to protect and feed them. Others tried to frighten them so they wouldn't run away. With some slaves, one or the other tactic worked, but as Sherman and his legions passed, people streamed away from their shacks and shanties, left the fields they knew so well, and followed him, as they might have followed Moses, come to lead them to the promised land.

Sherman's march might be imagined as an orderly advance of men in smart blue uniforms, but such was not the case. Having lived off the land and slept wherever they could find a place—in a hayloft or a shack—Sherman's soldiers were a raggle-taggle bunch. A reporter for the New York *Tribune* wrote, "The procession of the vehicles and animals was of the most grotesque description. There were donkeys, large and small, almost smothered under burdens of turkeys, geese and other kinds of poultry." There were "old sulkies, farm wagons and buggies, hacks, chaises, rockaways, aristocratic and family carriages, all filled with plunder and provisions—bacon, hams, potatoes, flour, pork, sorghum, and freshly slaughtered pigs and sheep dangling from saddle, tree and wagon, enough, one would suppose, to feed the army for a fortnight."

Joining in this strange procession were several thousand fugitives from slavery, dressed in clothes taken from the empty houses of their masters and mistresses: swallowtailed coats, tall silk hats, threadbare trousers, tattered skirts, and straw hats decorated with bright streamers. People came with all their children, with their meager hoards of worldly goods; and when Sherman's columns

Here, a group of Sherman's veterans pose for an unknown photographer. *National Archives*

were attacked, those few who were armed or could borrow firearms helped to defend the soldiers who had come to set them free. These people trusted Sherman, and when they came to visit him, he took time to talk to them. It was said that he put them at their ease and did not talk down to them. It is an irony that the Union general slaves most loved was a man who was not an abolitionist but nonetheless led a march the likes of which had been envisioned years before by John Brown and Frederick Douglass.

Because of Sherman's capture of Atlanta, doubts about who would win the war were put to rest. A Union victory was in the air, and Lincoln's growing popularity—together with mistakes made by the Democrats, not the least of which was their nomination of McClellan as their presidential candidate—spelled out a victory for Lincoln in his bid for reelection.

On November 8, 1864, Lincoln won by a wide margin, garnering 212 out of 233 electoral votes.

The result of the presidential election served as an early Christmas present for black people. Letters of congratulation came to Lincoln from all sections of the country, some of them from former slaves. On December 25, Edgar Dinsmore, serving in the Fifty-Fourth, wrote to his fiancée in New York, "We are glad to know that President Lincoln is reelected. It gives us renewed hope and makes us eager to meet the foe."

After Lincoln's death, Douglass wrote that his reelection had "silenced in a good degree the discontent felt at the length of the war and the complaints of it being an abolition war." He wrote, "Since William the Silent, who was the soul of the mighty war for religious liberty against Spain and the Spanish inquisition, no leader of men has been more loved and trusted in such generous measures as was Abraham Lincoln."

Lincoln knew that his Emancipation Proclamation was effective only as a war measure, that in peacetime it might be invalidated. On the other hand, he knew that an amendment to the Constitution abolishing slavery—if passed in both houses of the Congress and ratified by the states—would be irreversible.

On December 6, in his message to the Congress, Lincoln said:

> At the last session of Congress a proposed amendment of the Constitution, abolishing slavery throughout the United States, passed the Senate, but failed for lack of the requisite two-thirds vote in the House of Representatives. Although the present is the same Congress, and nearly the same members, and without questioning the wisdom or patriotism of those who stood in opposition, I venture to recommend the reconsideration and passage of the measure at the pressent session.*

By the end of January, Arkansas, Louisiana, Maryland, and Missouri had abolished slavery; and on January 31, in response to widespread sentiment and at

---

*In order to become law, a proposed amendment to the Constitution must pass in the Senate and the House of Representatives with the approval of two-thirds of the members in each body. It must be thereafter ratified by three-quarters of the states.

Lincoln's further urging, the Thirteenth Amendment passed in the House. When the decision was announced, bedlam ruled in the crowded galleries and halls and in the surrounding streets. As was the day of the issuance of the Emancipation Proclamation two years before, this day was marked by the firing of one hundred cannon.*

Charles A. Dana, who had helped shepherd the amendment through the Congress, later praised the President's astuteness: "Lincoln was a supreme politician. He understood politics because he understood human nature. . . . He was all solid, hard, keen intelligence combined with goodness."

The day after the triumph, a military band led an admiring crowd to the White House. Lincoln stood out on a balcony and spoke briefly. He praised his own state of Illinois for becoming the first to ratify the amendment and praised Maryland for acting swiftly. He said he hoped for peace and restoration of the Union.

March 4, 1865, was a wet and windy day. The inaugural procession was much like the one four years before; but this time, the mud on Pennsylvania Avenue was twice as deep. The dome of the Capitol was finished, crowned appropriately by a statue representing freedom.

The demands of leadership in the war, the

This cartoon, "Long Abraham Lincoln a Little Longer," indicating Lincoln's growing popularity, appeared in *Harper's Weekly* following his reelection. *Williams College Sawyer Library*

---

*The Thirteenth Amendment was, at last, ratified on December 6, 1865.

tragedy of Willie's death, and the constant worry over Mary's mental instability had left their mark on the tormented president. He still could grasp an ax by the end of its handle and hold it extended at right angles to his body, but his face was that of a much older, wiser man.

As he stood up to speak, a shaft of sunlight was released by the almost impenetrable bank of clouds that hung above the city. His face, we are told, was suddenly illuminated, as if at an angel's beckoning.

As was his habit, he put on his spectacles. He glanced at a printed copy of his speech, then, as he began to speak, he looked out at the crowd standing on the level ground below him.

> On the occasion corresponding to this four years ago, all thoughts were anxiously directed to an impending civil war. All dreaded it. All sought to avert it. While the inaugural address was being delivered from this place, devoted altogether to *saving* the Union without war, insurgent agents were in the city seeking to *destroy* it without war—seeking to dissolve the Union. . . . Both parties deprecated war; but one of them would *make* war rather than let the nation survive; and the other would *accept* war rather than let it perish. And the war came.
>
> One eighth of the whole population were colored slaves, not distributed generally over the Union, but localized in the Southern part of it. These slaves constituted a peculiar and powerful interest. All knew that this interest was, somehow, the cause of the war. It may seem strange that any men should dare to ask a just God's assistance in wringing their bread from the sweat of other men's faces; but let us judge not that we be not judged.

Then, as he seldom had before, he sounded like a vengeful preacher:

> Fondly do we hope—fervently do we pray—that this mighty scourge of war may speedily pass away. Yet, if God wills that it continue, until all

the wealth piled by the bond-man's two hundred and fifty years of unrequited toil shall be sunk, and until every drop of blood drawn with the lash, shall be paid for by another drawn with the sword, as was said three thousand years ago, so still it must be said "the judgements of the Lord are true and righteous altogether."

His clarity of mind and profound humanity enabled him to see beyond the tragedy of war:

With malice toward none; with charity for all; with firmness in the right, as God gives us to see the right, let us strive to finish the work we are in; to bind up the nation's wounds; to care for him who shall have borne the battle, and for his widow, and his orphan—to do all which may achieve and cherish a just and a lasting peace among ourselves, and with all nations.

Here, at last, with victory all but assured, Lincoln had felt free to express his outrage over slavery. Here, a vision of the private man began to merge with an image of a president who had always at least tried to separate his emotions from his duty to the law.

A reception at the White House followed the inauguration ceremonies. Frederick Douglass was by then a friend of Lincoln. Lincoln had consulted with him and had always treated him with extraordinary warmth and courtesy. Accordingly, Douglass went to the White House to attend the gathering. As he approached the designated door, one of two guards told him that no person of his color was allowed to enter. Douglass, determined to gain entry, told the guard that no such order could have come from Lincoln. At last, Douglass told someone who recognized him to announce him, and as soon as Lincoln sent an order to admit him, he went in. Douglass remembered, "Mr. Lincoln stood in his grand simplicity and *home-like beauty*. Recognizing me, even before I reached him, he exclaimed, so that all around could hear him, 'Here comes my friend Douglass.'"

Douglass greeted him and shook his hand. Lincoln said, "I am glad to see you. I saw you in the crowd to-day, listening to my inaugural address. How did you like it?"

"Mr. Lincoln, I must not detain you. . . ."

"No, no. You must stop a little, Douglass. There is no man in the country whose opinion I value more than yours. I want to know what you think. . . ."

Douglass answered, "Mr. Lincoln, that was a sacred effort."

Lincoln lived just long enough to witness the defeat of the Confederacy. Slowly, with the help of dozens of black regiments, Grant had reversed Union fortunes in Virginia. The weight that had settled on Lee's shoulders after Gettysburg had become a crushing burden.

As the Confederacy began to crumble in Virginia, Sherman's troops took Savannah, then swept northward. Sherman—interested only in what he called "vital points"—didn't waste his time on Charleston. "Charleston will fall by itself," he said, and he went on and sacked Columbia, South Carolina's capital.

The crews of warships flying the stars and stripes and manned by black as well as white Union sailors occupied batteries and strongholds guarding Charleston Harbor, including the redoutable Fort Sumter. With all Confederate guns secured, Lieutenant Colonel A. G. Bennett—commanding the Twenty-First Regiment United States Colored Troops—rowed into Charleston and demanded the surrender of the city, much of which had been set afire by Confederate soldiers under orders from General Pierre Gustave Toutant de Beauregard.

When the surrender was forthcoming, Bennett promised, "My command will render every possible assistance to your well-disposed citizens in extinguishing the flames."

The first conquerors to march along Charleston's charred and ruined thoroughfares and to give their services as firefighters were elements of Bennett's regiment. They were followed closely by two companies of the celebrated Massachusetts Fifty-Fourth.

For the black citizens of Charleston, this was a time to rejoice. A reporter from New England asked a woman, "You are glad the Yankees are come, then?"

"Oh, child," she said, "I can't bless the Lord enough. But I doesn't call you Yankees. I call you Jesus's aids. . . ." She reserved her highest praise for Lincoln. "And I call your head man the Messiah!"

Shortly after the arrival of black troops, doctor, editor, and writer Major Martin R. Delany came to Charleston to establish a recruiting office. Delany, who had been commissioned only weeks before, had become the ranking black man in the Union Army. A huge congregation of black people, freed by the occupation of the city, honored him at Zion Church, where he was the object of great admiration, not to mention curiosity.

Massachusetts abolitionist and women's rights activist Wendell Phillips wrote about the shame and sorrow of the city's white patricians—some of

The ruins of Charleston, South Carolina. Union soldiers, many of them members of black regiments, helped put out fires in Charleston, most of which had been set by retreating Southerners. *National Archives*

whose forebears had signed the Constitution: "Can you conceive a bitterer drop that God's chemistry could mix for a son of [South Carolina] than that a Massachusetts flag and a colored regiment should take possession of Charleston?"

Having burned Columbia, Sherman took his legions to North Carolina, where General Joseph E. Johnston—called by one historian a "jaunty little Game-Cock"—had been assigned by Lee to do what little he could do to keep Sherman occupied. Johnston's effort was to prove altogether fruitless.*

As we have seen, Lincoln and his son Tad went to Richmond April 4. They spent one night in that city, then began their voyage home. Aboard the *River Queen*, en route to Washington, Lincoln indulged in one of his few pastimes. To his guests aboard the steamer, he read passages from Shakespeare. The lament of Macbeth—who had murdered Duncan I of Scotland so that he could rule his kingdom—would long echo in the memories of the few who heard him read it.

> *Duncan is in his grave:*
> *After Life's fitful fever he sleeps well,*
> *Treason has done his worst; nor steel, nor poison,*
> *Malice domestic, foreign levy, nothing*
> *Can touch him further.*

One of Lincoln's listeners was a young French nobleman, the Marquis de Chambrun, who noted that, as Lincoln finished reading, he became reflective, then "began to explain to us how true a description of the murderer that one was; when the dark deed is achieved, its tortured perpetrator came to envy the sleep of his victim."

---

*Johnston—with 18,000 infantry against Sherman's 80,000—soon saw that it was time to quit; on April 17, he met Sherman in a little cabin near Durham Station, North Carolina, where they talked about a general peace. They met again on April 18 and negotiated terms much too liberal to suit Secretary of War Stanton, who, following Lincoln's death, felt free to repudiate them.

The *River Queen* docked in Washington on April 9, in the evening. That same day, while the steamer was approaching Washington, Lee had surrendered to Grant at Appomattox Courthouse, in Virginia.

Thanks to the generosity and foresight of both Grant and Lee, there was little bitterness at Appomattox. Before their meeting, Grant had sent word to Lee that he hoped that "all our difficulties may be settled without the loss of another life."

Lee, wanting none of the guerilla warfare that would follow the dispersal of his troops without surrender, met Grant in a tidy, red brick house, where they ended their long, bloody conflict. The terms, suggested by the president, were more generous than the ones recommended by several vengeful members

Robert E. Lee in 1865. Lee was a brilliant and aggressive soldier and, in 1865, despite reversals at the hands of Union generals, he became commander-in-chief of the Confederate armies. *National Archives*

of his cabinet. Lee's soldiers were allowed to go straight home. His officers and enlisted cavalrymen were allowed to keep their pistols and their horses.

That night, when news of Lee's surrender reached Washington, people shouted in the streets. Some fired pistols at the sky. At dawn, the booming of the cannon at the navy yard shook the city. Crowds gathered at the White House, and Lincoln, giving in to their demand, followed Tad to a window. Bands had gathered in the yard, and he asked them to play "Dixie," saying that it was his favorite tune.

For three days, the people of the city celebrated. On April 11, Lincoln gave his last public address. Knowing that he planned to speak, people started gathering at noon—some bringing picnic baskets filled with food, flasks of liquor, packs of cards.

By evening, an enormous throng had gathered. The yellow light of lamps and candles shimmered in the windows of the houses and the public buildings. A city that, for four years, had been threatened with invasion was at last a safe haven, or seemed so. As Lincoln's silhouette appeared in a second-story window, he was greeted by a sea of upturned faces and wave after wave of cheers.

Most people in the crowd wanted a triumphant affirmation of a victory over a rebellious Southern people, a people they had tried to think of as their enemy. They wanted a speech full of pride and bluster, but there was neither bitterness nor a sense of triumph in the president.

He had had two full days to think about the staggering reality of the military victory. A speech about responsibility and toil was not at all what the people hoped to hear, but he thought more about the work that lay ahead of him than the fading of the cheers of the multitude that stretched across the lawns and thoroughfares of his nation's capital.

He said, "We meet this evening not in sorrow, but in gladness of heart. The evacuation of Petersburg and Richmond, and the surrender of the principal insurgent army, give hope of a righteous and speedy peace. . . ."

As Lincoln finished reading the first page and went on to the next, he dropped the first page on the floor, where Tad picked it up and asked insistently for the next one. But Lincoln read without apparent interruption.

He reminded those who listened that, in his annual message to the Congress delivered on December 8, 1863,

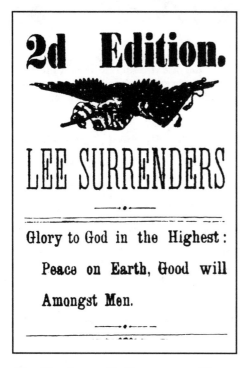

Headline from a Northern paper. *The collection of the author*

he had congratulated states that had voluntarily set their slaves free, and in a related proclamation, he had outlined a plan for reconstruction that would bring Southern states back into what he called "their proper practical relation with the Union." Included in this plan was a suggestion that freed slaves be educated while apprenticed to professionals or artisans.

A small portion of the population of Louisiana had voted that their state return to the Union, as a free state. Lincoln urged support for the Louisiana government, though it couldn't rightly be called representative. The framers of its constitution had included his suggestions. They had given people of the state "the benefit of public schools equally to black and white" and had given qualified black men the vote. Lincoln saw Louisiana as a possible example. "What has been said of Louisiana will apply to other states."

He noted that the validity and structure of the Louisiana government had recently been criticized. "The question is, will it be wiser to take it as it is and help to improve it, or to reject and disperse it?"

He hoped, he said, that the Congress, and the courts—if need be—would support the Louisiana effort. Not to do so would be tantamount to telling the white Southern citizen, "You are worthless or worse; we will neither help you, nor be helped by you." Not to do so, he suggested, would amount to telling the black citizen, "This cup of liberty which these, your old masters, hold to your lips we will dash from you, and leave you to the chances of gathering the spilled and scattered contents. . . ." He went on to say that black people, seeing all united for them, would be "inspired with vigilance, and energy, and daring. . . ."

The address was disappointing to an audience that was hoping for a victory speech. Some people left while he was speaking. Others talked or listened listlessly. Lincoln finished, waved, and backed away from the window. He gathered up the pages of his manuscript and, with Tad at his side, left the room with a sense of having spoken from his heart but having failed his audience.

Mary Lincoln's dressmaker, Elizabeth Keckley, had, for four years, been a friend and confidante. A few weeks earlier, Mary had told Keckley, "Poor Mr.

Bust of Lincoln by Max Bachmann, finished in 1905. *Williams College Sawyer Library*

Lincoln is looking so broken-hearted, so worn out, I fear he will not get through the next four years."

Lincoln was, indeed, close to exhaustion. He needed time off and, against the advice of members of his cabinet—especially Stanton—and against the counsel of his bodyguards, planned to go to a play at Ford's Theater on the evening of April 14.

On the way to the theater, the Lincolns drove through a thick fog. The ruts in the muddy streets glistened in the blur of lamplight. A small crowd greeted them at the doors of the theater. They went in and climbed a stairway to a box that overlooked the stage.

During the third act of *Our American Cousin*, Lincoln was shot, from behind, by John Wilkes Booth, a man so irrational that he had failed to recognize that the Confederacy had been defeated and that slavery was dead and could never rise again.

It turned out that the shooting of the president was central to a plot in which the other targets were Seward and the recently installed vice president, Andrew Johnson. Seward was severely wounded but survived. Johnson was spared when his would-be assassin lost his nerve.

Lincoln, who never regained consciousness, was put to bed in a modest little house across the street from the theater. The people of a city who, three days before, had celebrated peace, were once again frightened of the shadows that had been pursuing them since the firing on Fort Sumter.

Lincoln died at 7:22 A.M., the morning after he was shot. One of the several doctors in attendance said, "The President is no more!"

How wrong the doctor was. Lincoln lived, and still lives, in the hearts of the men and women of America and is honored the world over. He had said that the Declaration of Independence had given "liberty not alone to the people of this country, but hope to all the world, for all future time." In an hour of great peril, Lincoln had preserved that liberty. Hating slavery as he always had and loving freedom as he did, he understood that, "in giving freedom to the *slave*, we assure freedom to the *free*—honorable alike in what we give, and what we preserve."

AFTERWORD

Elizabeth Keckley—who, though her skin was light, identified herself as black—had spent many days and a few nights in the Lincoln White House. Mary Lincoln called her "Lizzie." Lincoln, who was very fond of her, had called her "Madame Elizabeth."

Following Lincoln's death, when Keckley went to Mary's bedroom, she found the Lincoln's elder son with Tad at the bedside of their grieving mother. "Robert was bending over his mother with tender affection, and little Tad was crouched at the foot of the bed with a world of agony on his young face."

Keckley went to view Lincoln's body:

> I lifted the whole cloth from the face of the man I had worshipped as an idol—looked up to as a demi-god. . . . There was something beautiful as well as grandly solemn in the expression on the placid face. There lurked the sweetness and gentleness of childhood, and the stately grandeur of god-like intellect. I gazed long at the face, and turned away with tears in

my eyes and a choking sensation in my throat. Ah! Never was a man so widely mourned before.

The response of most black people to Lincoln's death was direct and unequivocal. As his body lay in state in Washington, a group of South Carolina freedmen drafted a resolution that began, "Resolved that we look upon the death of the Chief Magistrate of our country as a national calamity, and an irrepressible loss beyond the power of words to express, covering the land with gloom and sorrow, mourning and desolation."

On April 21, 1865, Lincoln's funeral train began its slow and solemn journey to his final resting place in Springfield, Illinois. Along the way, black people in villages and towns and great cities wept for their fallen leader. In the cities, Lincoln's casket was pulled slowly through the streets and thoroughfares.

The Reverend J. Sella Martin—pastor of New York's First Colored Presbyterian Church—saw it as a mark of what had still to be accomplished that black soldiers who had served in Union regiments were at first denied the right to march in the funeral procession with their white counterparts. After the federal government stepped in and asked that the black veterans be allowed to join in the solemnities, they were made to walk so far behind that they never even saw the hearse.

Years later, Frederick Douglass, who still thought of Lincoln as having been a "white man's President," was nonetheless able to compare him to the founding fathers. Douglass said,

> It was a great thing to achieve American independence when we numbered three millions, but it was a greater thing to save this country from dismemberment and ruin when it numbered thirty millions. He alone of all our Presidents was to have the opportunity to destroy slavery, and to lift into manhood millions of his countrymen hitherto held as chattels and numbered among the beasts of the field.

BIBLIOGRAPHICAL ESSAY AND NOTES ON SOURCES

The notes that follow this essay refer to histories of the Civil War. Of the several hundred such books readily available, I have listed only some of those by Bruce Catton, Henry Steele Commager, Shelby Foote, and James M. McPherson. I have also chosen to include Winston S. Churchill's *The American Civil War*—taken from the author's monumental *History of the English Speaking Peoples*. To these general works, I have added Edmund Wilson's *Patriotic Gore: Studies in the Literature of the American Civil War.*

The seven-volume *A Documentary History of the Negro People in the United States,* the earliest of such works, was highly praised by the distinguished black historian and sociologist W. E. B. Du Bois. It was an important source. See Aptheker. Lerone Bennett's *Before the Mayflower* was another helpful history.

Six books listed in the bibliography are concerned exclusively with black people and the Civil War. These are the works of Dudley Taylor Cornish, Joseph T. Glatthaar, James G. Hollandsworth, James M. McPherson, Benjamin Quarles, and William Wells Brown. The first three are largely military histories. McPherson, Quarles, and Brown deal also with matters social and political.

The Black Abolitionist Papers, edited by Ripley, et al., rate a separate paragraph. The first four volumes gave me mostly background information. The fifth volume, which covers black opinion in the United States from 1849 to 1865, was especially useful.

Of the many works by and about Frederick Douglass, the most important are the autobiographies. Of the several good biographies of Douglass, I have listed those by Dickson, Foner, and McFeely.

Hundreds of Lincoln scholars have interpreted and reinterpreted Lincoln papers now available on microfilm. Because I made no attack whatsoever on these sources, I relied heavily on the efforts of the best biographers: David Herbert Donald, Mark E. Neely, James G. Randall, Carl Sandburg, and Benjamin P. Thomas.

Since Lincoln's friend and law partner William H. Herndon drew so much on memory, it seems to me that he belongs in a separate category from the above biographers. Many other people who knew Lincoln have given us at least the flavor of the great man's thought and conversation, but, had it not been for the unsentimental Herndon, we would not know Lincoln as we do.

As its title indicates, *Lincoln and the Negro* by Benjamin Quarles occupies a special place among biographies of Lincoln.

My most important sources were Lincoln's own recorded speeches, orders, proclamations, letters, notes, and memos, as found in the 1894 edition of the complete works of Abraham Lincoln, as preserved and edited by Lincoln's secretaries, John G. Nicolay and John Hay, and the 1953 collected works of Abraham Lincoln, as edited by Basler.

In presenting physical descriptions of Lincoln and his contemporaries and the places where they lived and worked, I made frequent use of photographs as they appear in books that are readily available. By far the best of these is the magnificent 1992 *Lincoln: An Illustrated Biography,* by three members of the Kunhardt family.

Rather than provide detailed annotation for this book, I here present a series of short essays on my sources—one for every chapter and one for the Afterword. This is not as casual a method as it might, at first, appear to be. These essays, together with the indexes in the volumes listed in my bibliography, provide clear links between my text and my sources.

CHAPTER 1: FATHER ABRAHAM IS COME!

Accounts of Lincoln's visit to Richmond vary widely and are often contradictory. In reconstructing Lincoln's arrival in what had been the Confederate capital, I referred to general histories and to the biographies. See especially Donald. In writing briefly as I did about New Salem, I relied on a visit to the site and on the biographies. Thomas wrote beautifully about Lincoln's early years. Having lived in New Orleans years ago, I was, I hope, able to evoke its atmosphere. In covering Lincoln's early interest in the law, I referred to Arthur Lehman Goodhart's speech titled "Lincoln and the Law," as it appears in *Lincoln and the Gettysburg Address,* edited by Nevins. Duff's book was indispensable. For Lovejoy, see Dillon.

CHAPTER 2: THE ROOT OF THE TROUBLES

My account of Lincoln's life at Mrs. Sprigg's boardinghouse and his term in the Congress was drawn from general works and the biographies. Donald was especially helpful. For the John Quincy Adams quote, see Tocqueville. See Nagel. See Kemble, edited by Scott. Nonviolent abolitionist William Lloyd Garrison is mentioned and is quoted here and in other places in this book. For biographies of Garrison, see Nye and Merrill.

CHAPTER 3: A CRIMINAL BETRAYAL

For accounts of Lincoln's years in Springfield, I referred to the biographies and to my notes on the city as it is today, especially its Lincoln sites: the Lincoln Home, the Lincoln-Herndon Law Offices, and the Old State Capitol. Herndon's recollections were invaluable. In writing about the two cases in which slavery was an issue, I referred to the biographies and to Duff. Some of the James Forten quotes appear in Douty's short biography. Other information on James Forten came to me from friend and scholar Julie Winch, who is working on a definitive biography of the black patriot and abolitionist. See also Burchard's *Charlotte Forten*.

CHAPTER 4: A UNIVERSAL FEELING

In contrasting Lincoln's character and his views with those of Stephen Douglas, I referred to the biographies of Lincoln and Johannsen's life of Douglas. In this chapter, I began to make wide use of the recorded statements of both men. The wonderful account of the Douglas utterance in Chicago's Public Square appears in Pierce's second volume. For early racial incidents in New York City, see Gilje. For riots in Philadelphia, Pennsylvania, see Du Bois. My account of the tribulations and the trial of Anthony Burns was taken from black histories and an 1854 pamphlet on the riot and the trial found in the Williams College Chapin Library. All Charlotte Forten quotes were taken from her journals. The story of the beating of Charles Sumner has been told, in one form or another, in most histories of the Civil War. The account in Garrison's *The Liberator* was taken from a microfilm edition of that paper.

CHAPTER 5: IN HIS PRISON HOUSE

The Dred Scott case has been discussed in a thousand or more books and articles. Good and reliable accounts of the case and discussions of its implications appear in the general works and in black histories. For a detailed discussion of the case, see Fehrenbacher. For the seven scheduled debates, see Nicolay and Hay, and Basler. Lively histories of the towns and cities in which the debates took place were written and edited by members of the Federal Writers Project of the Works Progress Administration of the State of Illinois. See Hansen. Also useful were two volumes in the series *Rivers of America.* See Gray. See Masters.

CHAPTER 6: SO SAD A FACE

As I wrote this chapter, I relied on Nicolay and Hay and on Basler. Comments on internal contradictions are my own. For accounts of John Brown's activities, see Du Bois, Foner, Oates, and Scott and Scott.

CHAPTER 7: RIGHT MAKES MIGHT

I relied on Herndon's memory for the dialogue about Lincoln's first trip to New York. My account of Lincoln's stay in New York City was drawn partly from my long study of the city's history. Incidentally, I have seen printed menus listing food available in 1860 at the Astor House. A study of the lives of many abolitionists enabled me to chronicle the participation of these people in the funding of Brown's raid on Harpers Ferry. For more on the Secret Six, see Renehan. Nat Turner's exploits are recounted in *The Fires of Jubilee,* by Oates. My sketch of the life of Toussaint L'Ouverture was taken from black histories, some of which are listed in the bibliography. For the political campaign of 1860, see Fite. See Pierce for a colorful account of the convention in Chicago. Responses of black people to the Lincoln nomination were gathered from black histories. For John Rock, see McPherson. For H. Ford Douglass, see Ripley's *The Black Abolitionist Papers,* volume 5. For Frederick Douglass, see Dickson, Douglass, Foner, and McFeely.

CHAPTER 8: THE MYSTIC CHORDS OF MEMORY

For Lincoln's good-bye to his partner, see Herndon. Accounts of Lincoln's farewell to his neighbors, his indecorous arrival in Washington, and his days as president-elect appear in many general works and in all responsible biographies. For the reaction of black leaders to the call for soldiers to defend the capital and for their responses to Lincoln's First Inaugural Address, including comments in the *Anglo-African,* see Quarles's *The Negro in the Civil War,* McPherson's *The Negro's Civil War,* and Ripley's *The Black Abolitionist Papers,* volume 5. Robert Gould Shaw was the private who provided a description of Lincoln and his sons greeting New York's Seventh Regiment. See Shaw. See Burchard.

CHAPTER 9: A TIME OF TIMES

For accounts of the circumstances that surrounded Lincoln's writing of the Emancipation Proclamation, see Franklin. This short work, together with general histories of the Civil

War and black histories in which the proclamation is discussed, enabled me to present what I hope is a fair sample of black and white, radical and conservative responses to the proclamation. For Sumner, see Donald's *Charles Sumner and the Rights of Man.* For accounts of McClellan's Peninsula campaign, see general histories. For Antietam, see general histories and see Sears. Robert Gould Shaw wrote the lines on the aftermath of battle. See Shaw and Burchard. Fremont's proclamation is discussed by McPherson, Quarles, and Donald, as is Hunter's proclamation. For details of Hunter's life, see Miller. Colonization is outlined in general histories, in biographies of Lincoln, and in black histories. Butler's initiatives in regard to contrabands and black participation in the Civil War are discussed at length in black histories and in Werlich. For Greeley's open letter, see Donald; and for Lincoln's answer, see Nicolay. Military and missionary activities in the Sea Islands of South Carolina are chronicled in Rose and in Forten's journals. Chiriquí and Isle à Vache are discussed by Quarles in *The Negro in the Civil War,* by McPherson in *The Negro's Civil War,* and in some of the biographies. Preacher Henry Turner's wonderful account of the reading of the proclamation as it appeared in *The Evening Star* can be found in McPherson's *The Negro's Civil War.*

CHAPTER 10: THE WORLD WILL LITTLE NOTE

The Pulitzer Prize–winning study *Lincoln at Gettysburg,* by Garry Wills, is, to date, the most penetrating work on Lincoln's Gettysburg Address. As does no other writer, historian, or political philosopher, Wills tells us why the address was so great a document. For purely physical descriptions of events preceding the delivery of the address and the events of November 19, 1863, at Gettysburg, I relied on Carr's 1906 memoir and on Phillip B. Kunhardt's highly pictorial *A New Birth of Freedom.* Of the seven essays—six of them texts of speeches—in *Lincoln and the Gettysburg Address,* edited by Nevins, the most useful were Nevins's introduction, Arthur Lehman Goodhart's speech, and Paul H. Douglas's remarks. The words of the father who went to Gettysburg to retrieve his son's remains may be found in Catton, volume 3. The opinion of an editor of the Chicago *Times* appears in Wills. The opinions of English and Scottish journalists appear in Carr. In his *Lincoln,* Donald describes Lincoln's illness.

CHAPTER 11: GET DOWN, YOU FOOL

The story of how Holmes warned Lincoln to climb down from the rampart at Fort Stevens has been repeated, in one form or another, many times. Some historians have called it fanciful. I have reason to believe it is not. Years after the event, Holmes told English academic Harold J. Laski that he had indeed so warned the president. See Woollcott. In Laski's version of the story, Holmes says, "Get down, you fool." Other versions have him saying, "Get down, you damn fool." As a young man, Holmes swore often, so the latter version may be accurate, but, finding no support for it, I reluctantly chose the former. In any case, we know that Lincoln did go twice to Fort Stevens and exposed himself to danger. Livermore's published work is included in my bibliography. The history of black participation in the Union Army is contained in the works of Cornish and Glatthaar. The touching Dumas quote may be found in Hollandsworth. For what was probably the first account of the bravery of Lieutenant Callioux, see Brown. For Shaw and the Fifty-Fourth, see Burchard, Forten, and Shaw. For the story of the draft riots in New York, in 1863, see Cook and the pamphlet mentioned in a footnote to the text. For an account of the Douglass interview with Lincoln, see Douglass. Various versions of the Fort Pillow massacre appear in Cornish, Glatthaar, McPherson, Quarles, and Brown.

CHAPTER 12: AFTER LIFE'S FITFUL FEVER

Sojourner Truth's visit to the White House is described in a letter by Truth to a friend of hers. See Truth. Sherman's statements ruling out black participation in his army, together with accounts of his campaigns, can be found in black histories and in general histories of the Civil War. Elias Smith's account of Sherman's march from Atlanta to the sea appears in *The Faber Book of Reportage,* edited by Carey. Douglass has provided us with accounts of his meetings with the president; see his *Life and Times.* Accounts of the occupation of Charleston, South Carolina, may be found in general histories and in Quarles's *The Negro in the Civil War.* An account of Lincoln's reading of Shakespeare—aboard the *River Queen*—appears in Donald's *Lincoln,* as does an account of the circumstances that surrounded the delivery of Lincoln's last public address. Keckley's reminiscences include Mary Lincoln's pessimistic comment about Lincoln's health. Reliable accounts of the shooting of the president are readily available. Interested as I am in Lincoln's life and his works, I gave as little space as possible to his assassination.

AFTERWORD

See Keckley. The story of the treatment of black soldiers in New York following Lincoln's death can be found in a letter written by the Reverend J. Sella Martin, as included in *The Black Abolitionist Papers,* volume 5. See Ripley. Douglass's remarks about Lincoln and his presidency are included in his *Life and Times.*

BIBLIOGRAPHY

Aptheker, Herbert, ed. *A Documentary History of the Negro People in the United States.* New York: Citadel Press, 1969.

Basler, Roy P., ed. *The Collected Works of Lincoln,* 9 vols. New Brunswick: Rutgers University Press, 1953–1955.

Bennett, Lerone, Jr. *Before the Mayflower: A History of the Negro in America, 1619–1964.* Chicago: Johnson Publishing, 1962.

Brown, William Wells. *The Negro in the American Rebellion.* New York: Citadel Press, 1971.

Burchard, Peter. *One Gallant Rush: Robert Gould Shaw and His Brave Black Regiment.* New York: St. Martin's Press, 1965.

———.*We'll Stand by the Union: Robert Gould Shaw and the Black 54th Massachusetts Regiment.* New York: Facts on File, 1993.

———. *Charlotte Forten: A Black Teacher in the Civil War.* New York: Crown Publishers, 1995.

Carey, John, ed. *The Faber Book of Reportage.* London: Faber & Faber, 1987.

Carr, Clark E. *Lincoln at Gettysburg.* Chicago: A. C. McClurg & Co., 1906.

Catton, Bruce. *The Centennial History of the Civil War,* 3 vols. Garden City: Doubleday & Co., 1961–1965.

Churchill, Winston S. *The American Civil War.* New York: Fairfax Press, 1985.

Commager, Henry Steele, ed. *The Blue and the Grey: The Story of the Civil War as Told by Participants.* Indianapolis: Bobbs-Merrill, 1950.

Cook, Adrian. *The Armies of the Streets: The New York City Draft Riots of 1863.* Lexington: University of Kentucky Press, 1974.

Cornish, Dudley Taylor. *The Sable Arm.* New York: Longmans Green & Co., 1956.

Dillon, Merton Lynn. *Elijah P. Lovejoy, Abolitionist Editor.* Urbana: University of Illinois Press, 1961.

Donald, David Herbert. *Charles Sumner and the Rights of Man.* New York: Alfred A. Knopf, 1970.

————. *Lincoln.* New York, London, Toronto, Sydney, Tokyo, and Singapore: Simon & Schuster, 1995.

Douglass, Frederick. *Autobiographies.* New York: Library of America, 1994. This single volume contains *Narrative of the Life of Frederick Douglass, an American Slave,* first published in 1845; *My Bondage and My Freedom,* first published in 1845; *Life and Times of Frederick Douglass,* first published in 1893.

Douty, Esther M. *Forten, the Sailmaker: Pioneer of Negro Rights.* Chicago: Rand McNally, 1968.

DuBois, W.E.B. *The Philadelphia Negro: A Social Study.* New York: Benjamin Blom, 1967.

————. *John Brown.* New York: International Publishers, 1968.

Duff, John J. *A. Lincoln: Prairie Lawyer.* New York: Rhinehart, 1960.

Fehrenbacher, Don Edward. *The Dred Scott Case: Its Significance in American Law and Politics.* New York: Oxford University Press, 1978.

Fite, Emerson David. *The Presidential Campaign of 1860.* New York: Macmillan, 1911.

Foner, Phillip S. *The Life and Writings of Frederick Douglass.* New York: International Publishers, 1950–1955.

Foote, Shelby. *The Civil War, a Narrative,* 2 vols. New York: Random House, 1958–1974.

Forten, Charlotte L. *The Journals of Charlotte Forten Grimke,* ed. Brenda Stevenson. New York: Oxford University Press, 1988.

Franklin, John Hope. *The Emancipation Proclamation.* Garden City: Doubleday & Co., 1963.

Gilje, Paul A. *The Road to Mobocracy: Popular Disorder in New York City, 1763–1834.* Chapel Hill and London: University of North Carolina Press, 1987.

Glatthaar, Joseph T. *Forged in Battle: The Civil War Alliance of Black Soldiers and White Officers.* New York: Free Press, 1990.

Gray, James. *The Illinois,* part of *The Rivers of America* series. New York: Farrar and Rinehart, 1940.

Hansen, Harry, ed. *Illinois: A Descriptive and Historical Guide.* New York: Hastings House, 1974. Compiled by the Federal Writers Project of the Works Progress Administration of the State of Illinois.

Herndon, William H. *The Hidden Lincoln, from the Letters and Papers of William H. Herndon,* ed. Emanuel Hertz. New York: Viking Press, 1938.

Herndon, William H., and Jesse W. Weik. *Abraham Lincoln: The True Story of a Great Life.* 2 vols. Chicago: Bedford, Clarke & Co., 1889.

Hollandsworth, James G. Jr. *The Louisiana Native Guards.* Baton Rouge and London: Louisiana State University Press, 1995.

Johannsen, Robert Walter. *Stephen A. Douglas.* New York: Oxford University Press, 1973.

Jones, Howard. *Mutiny on the Amistad: The Saga of a Slave Revolt and Its Impact on American Abolition, Law, and Diplomacy.* New York: Oxford University Press, 1986.

Keckley, Elizabeth. *Behind the Scenes, or Thirty Years a Slave, and Four Years in the White House.* New York: Oxford University Press, 1988.

Kemble, Frances Anne. *Journal of a Residence on a Georgian Plantation in 1838–1839,* ed. and with an introduction by John Anthony Scott. New York: Alfred A. Knopf, 1961.

Kunhardt, Philip B. Jr. *A New Birth of Freedom: Lincoln at Gettysburg.* Boston: Little Brown, 1983.

Kunhardt, Philip B. Jr., Philip B. Kunhardt III, and Peter W. Kunhardt. *Lincoln: An Illustrated Biography.* New York: Alfred A. Knopf, 1992.

Livermore, George A. *An Historical Research Respecting the Opinions of the Founders of the Republic, on Negroes as Slaves, as Citizens, and as Soldiers.* New York: Arno Press, 1969.

Masters, Edgar Lee. *The Sangamon,* part of *The Rivers of America* series. New York: Farrar & Rinehart, 1942.

McFeely, William S. *Frederick Douglass.* New York and London: W. W. Norton & Co., 1991.

McPherson, James M. *The Negro's Civil War: How American Negroes Felt and Acted during the War for the Union.* New York: Pantheon Books, 1965.

————. *Battle Cry of Freedom: The Civil War Era.* New York: Oxford University Press, 1988.

Merrill, Walter M. *Against Wind and Tide: A Biography of William Lloyd Garrison.* Cambridge: Harvard University Press, 1963.

Miller, Edward A. *Lincoln's Abolitionist General: The Biography of David Hunter.* Columbia: University of South Carolina Press, 1997.

Nagel, Paul C. *John Quincy Adams: A Public Life, a Private Life.* New York: Alfred A. Knopf, 1997.

Neely, Mark E. *The Last Best Hope of Earth: Abraham Lincoln and the Promise of America.* Cambridge: Harvard University Press, 1993.

Nevins, Allan. *Lincoln and the Gettysburg Address.* Urbana: University of Illinois Press, 1964.

Nicolay, John G. and John Hay, eds. *Abraham Lincoln: Complete Works, Comprising His Speeches, Letters, State Papers, and Miscellaneous Writings.* New York: Century Co., 1894.

Nye, Russell Blaine. *William Lloyd Garrison and the Humanitarian Reformers.* Boston: Little Brown, 1955.

Oates, Stephen B. *The Fires of Jubilee: Nat Turner's Fierce Rebellion.* New York: Harper & Row, 1975.

————. *To Purge This Land with Blood: A Biography of John Brown.* Amherst: University of Massachusetts Press, 1984.

Pierce, Bessie Louise. *A History of Chicago,* 3 vols. New York: Alfred A. Knopf, 1937–1957.

Preston, Dickson J. *Young Frederick Douglass: The Maryland Years.* Baltimore: Johns Hopkins University Press, 1980.

Quarles, Benjamin. *Frederick Douglass.* Washington: Associated Publishers, 1948.

————. *The Negro in the Civil War.* Boston: Little Brown & Co., 1953.

————. *Lincoln and the Negro.* New York: Oxford University Press, 1962.

Randall, James G. *Lincoln the President,* 4 vols. New York: Dodd, Mead & Co., 1945–1955.

Renehan, Edward J. *The Secret Six: The True Tale of the Men Who Conspired with John Brown.* New York: Crown Publishers, 1995.

Ripley, Peter, et al., eds. *The Black Abolitionist Papers.* 5 vols. Chapel Hill: University of North Carolina Press, 1985–1992.

Rose, Willie Lee Nichols. *Rehearsal for Reconstruction: The Port Royal Experiment.* Indianapolis: Bobbs-Merrill, 1964.

Sandburg, Carl. *Abraham Lincoln: The Prairie Years.* 2 vols. New York: Harcourt Brace & Co., 1926.

————. *Abraham Lincoln: The War Years.,* 4 vols. New York: Harcourt Brace & Co., 1939.

Scott, John Anthony, and Robert Alan Scott. *John Brown of Harpers Ferry.* New York: Facts on File, 1988.

Sears, Stephen W. *Landscape Turned Red: The Battle of Antietam.* New Haven: Ticknor & Fields, 1983.

Shaw, Robert Gould. *Blue-Eyed Child of Fortune: The Civil War Letters of Robert Gould Shaw,* ed. and with an introduction by Russell Duncan. Athens: University of Georgia Press, 1992.

Stowe, Harriet Beecher. *Uncle Tom's Cabin: or Life Among the Lowly.* Boston: John P. Jewett & Co., 1852.

Thomas, Benjamin P. *Abraham Lincoln: A Biography.* New York: Alfred A. Knopf, 1954.

Tocqueville, Alexis de. *Journey to America.* New Haven: Yale University Press, 1960.

Truth, Sojourner. *Narrative of Sojourner Truth,* as told to her friend Olive Gilbert; published privately in 1878 and several times thereafter. See the edition with an introduction by Jeffery C. Stewart. New York: Oxford University Press, 1991.

Werlich, Robert. *"Beast" Butler: The Incredible Career of Major General Benjamin Franklin Butler.* Washington, DC: Quaker Press, 1962.

Wills, Garry. *Lincoln at Gettysburg: The Words That Remade America.* New York: Simon & Schuster, 1992.

Wilson, Edmund. *Patriotic Gore: Studies in the Literature of the American Civil War.* New York: Oxford University Press, 1962.

Woollcott, Alexander. *Long, Long Ago.* New York: Viking Press, 1943.

INDEX